"For an outsider who has always assumed that he was particularly aware of what was going on in the periphery, the first volume of *Asian Architects* is an overwhelming and refreshing surprise, not only because it features the work of architects one has never heard of, but also because it reveals the presence of a "regional" architecture of exceptional quality. As opposed to the Western world that largely oscillates between high-tech instrumentality and the spectacular, Asia mounts a diversity of expression that cuts across such categories in vigorous ways. Thus while on the one hand we find Sumet Jumsai's dramatic profiles standing out against the everyday horizon, on the other we encounter the careful *répétition differente* of the local vernacular as this may be found in Wu Liangyong's and C. Anjalendran's reinterpretation of Chinese and Sri Lankan domestic traditions. All of this comes to be mixed with the extraordinary richness of Balkrishna Doshi's Indian architecture as this has evolved over a lifetime and the sophisticated, all but classic, modernity of Korean Min Hyunsik's Sindo-Ricoh Factory of 1994. Where Sen Kapadia introduces a fresh modus into Indian architecture as abstract and symbolic as it is ecological, Sonny Chan Sau Yan is preoccupied with strong morphologies and with the projection of a skeletal architecture that is appropriate to the hot, wet climate of Singapore. Where Kapadia lies close to Barragan and Legoretta, Sonny Chan seems to approach the high-technology of Foster. What is striking about this opening anthology is the way many young Asian architects seem to have gone beyond the aporia of "post-coloniality" to create a subtly differentiated, trans-global, architecture that is equal to the best being produced anywhere."

Kenneth Frampton

ASian
architects

LEON VAN SCHAIK

WILLIAM S. W. LIM

SUMET JUMSAI

JIMMY C. S. LIM

WU LIANG YONG

BALKRISHNA DOSHI

MIN HYUNSIK

C. ANJALENDRAN

SARDJONO SANI

SEN KAPADIA

HU SHYR-FONG

MATHAR BUNNAG

SONNY CHAN SAU YAN

With a Foreword by Fumihiko Maki

Asian architects

1

Editor
Tan Kok Meng

SELECT
BOOKS

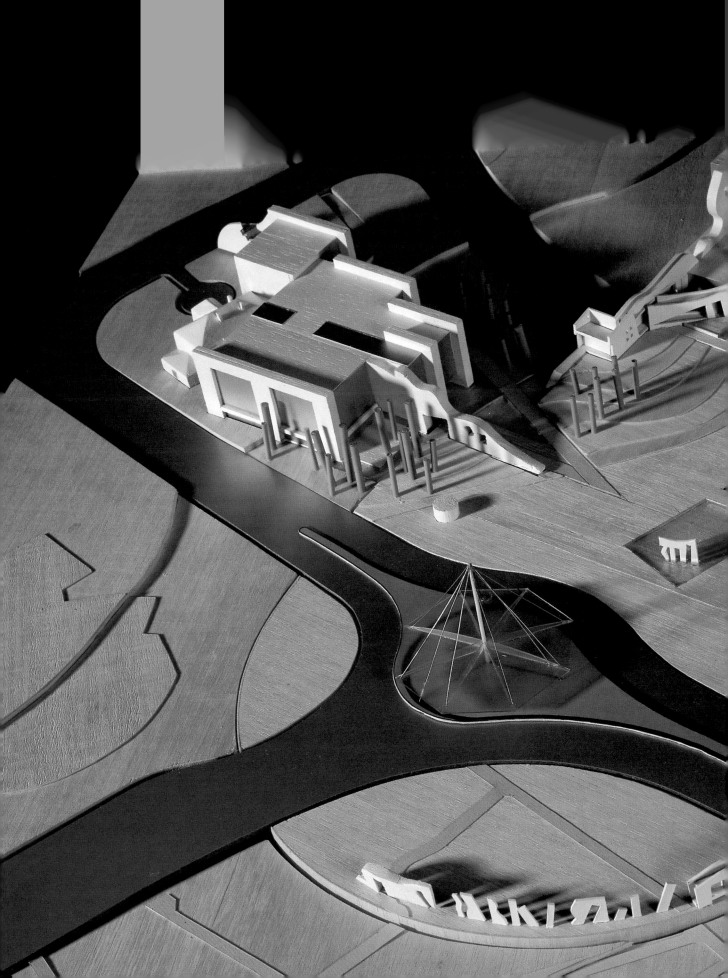

Cover picture: Husain-Doshi Gufa, Ahmedabad, India, 1993, by Balkrishna Doshi.
Frontispieces:
Pages 4 & 5: Ensemble of the proposed Place des Nations, Geneva, Switzerland, 1995, by Sumet Jumsai.
Pages 10 & 11: Kandawgyi Palace Hotel, Yangon, Myanmar, 1996, by Mathar Bunnag.
Endpaper design by Richard Hassell.

Asia witnessed a remarkable political, economic and social transformation in the post-war years. Many countries have progressed from agrarian-based colonial territories to independent nations with fast-growth industrial economies. This development is paralleled most evidently in the built environment, dramatically transforming the cityscapes of many Asian cities.

Notwithstanding the present economic turbulence in Asia, its rapid economic growth has also ushered in a shift in the balance of power along cultural lines. There is widely in place a confident affirmation of the cultural content of its indigenous societies and a coming to terms with its colonial pasts. Architecture, when understood as the production of cultural ideas in spatial terms, resolutely locates itself in such positions.

The Asian Architects series attempts to record this physical and thus cultural/aesthetic transformation and tries to reveal the creative processes that produced it. The series documents the creative works of Asian architects or architects working in the Asian context, whose works deserve a wider international exposure. As the material that is currently available is inadequate, dispersed, or not readily available, this series aims to be a primary source of information about architecture in Asia upon which further research can be conducted. Finally, it

Publisher's Preface

hopes to set the tone for sharpening architectural discourse and critical appreciation of architecture in Asia.

The series has an Advisory Committee comprising leading Asian architects. They are: Charles Correa, Tao Ho, Sumet Jumsai, William S. W. Lim, Fumihiko Maki, Leon van Schaik and Wu Liangyong.

The publishers are also guided by a Working Committee in Singapore, comprising William S. W. Lim, Mok Wei Wei, Robert Powell and Tan Kok Meng. Guest editors are invited to work on different volumes.

One of the major problems encountered was to define the parameters of such a series. What are the imaginary boundaries that the term Asia encompasses? What criteria should be used for the inclusion or exclusion of certain architects or works of architecture? Albeit potentially inviting controversy, for the purpose of manageability this series covers geographical bounds from Turkey in the west, to the Philippines in the east, from South Korea in the north to Australia in the south.

The inclusion of Australia in this series is somewhat timely. Sharing a common "post-colonial" experience with places like Malaysia, Singapore, India and Indonesia, Australia, in recent years, has continually looked askance at traditional sources of cultural influence from Europe and North America, to examine from within, authentic sources of its own physical and cultural experiences. Leon van Schaik, a South African born, British trained, Australian

academic, writing about his own particular experience in this series has made claims for a vital dialectical relationship between what he calls the "Metropolis" and the "Province". These terms correspond respectively to the predominant spheres of architectural discourse and those from the subordinate hinterlands. The flow of ideas from the "Metropolis" to the "Province" is not the conventionally regarded unilateral one, but encompasses a complex interconnectivity that distresses simple reduction. Framed in this way, Australia clearly sites itself in the "Province" together with the rest of Asia. It is this shared concern for exerting a concerted effort together with their Asian counterparts to offer alternative discourses that Australian architects are firmly aligned with the Asians in this series.

Japan, however, is excluded from the first six volumes of this series. It is felt that it has emerged over the years as a major source of architectural discourse through its high standard of professional achievement and its reputable international publications which include extensive documentation of Japanese works of architecture.

Each of the six volumes will feature the works and thoughts of leading Asian architects whose bodies of work are well respected by the architectural community at large. Also included are younger architects whose works show much promise. Twelve architects will be featured in each volume. Their selection for publication is purely contrived to bring together a good mix of unique approaches from different geographical regions.

The series also discusses what are perceived as important issues/topics confronting architecture and urbanism in Asia with the aim to provoke discussion. They are:

- The metropolis and province
- Writing post-coloniality
- Sustainable architecture
- Contemporary vernacular
- The new Asian architecture and urbanism
- Modernity and tradition

The publishers had the wholehearted support of the Advisory Committee, and benefited from their wise counsel on the contents and direction of the series. Meetings with the Working Committee were always long, demanding, challenging and rewarding. The publishers record their thanks and appreciation to every member of both committees for their invaluable contributions in making this a meaningful publishing experience, and this series a reality. And to the contributing architects, thank you for your willingness to be a part of this series and your patience in meeting our constant calls for additional materials.

Select Books is indeed pleased and privileged to be able to add to the growing literature on architecture in Asia.

Select Books

The production of architecture in rapidly urbanising Asia necessarily involves a double burden. On the one hand, design methodologies, construction processes and materials are intrinsically "modern". On the other, there exists an overwhelming weight of tradition and culture bearing down on Asian situations. Caught in this double bind, the easy way out would be to privilege one set of conditions over the other. However, such a simple resolution further dichotomises perceived differences between binary terms such as "tradition and modernity", "east and west".

In this first volume of the *Asian Architects* series, the diversity of approaches and attempts to consciously reflect upon this double burden is thus to be cherished. From the modernist strands of Hu Shyr-Fong, Min Hyun-Sik, Sardjono Sani and Sonny Chan; to the reconfiguration of specific cultures in contemporary terms in the works of Jimmy Lim, Sen Kapadia, C. Anjalendran and Wu Liangyong; we observe variously, syncretism, conflation and translation of the modern and the traditional, the "international" and the specific. The eclecticism of Mathar Bunnag; the affliation to avant-gardist art movements in Sumet Jumsai; to the synthesis of idea and form in Balkrishnan Doshi; further extend the debate beyond these "battle" lines, to embroil it in modern architectural traditions.

Editor's Note

These multiplicitous attitudes towards the contemporary Asian condition confirm the impression that architecture in Asia is indeed saturated with a pluralistic bewilderment.

When confronted with this pluralism, the prudent way to present it would be to let these diverse voices speak up from their own corners in their specific conditions as far as possible. Thus these are the positions that we are interested to reveal here; and this we have accommodated with a more fluid sort of graphic layout, yet still possessing a certain structure that aims to capture a notion of commonality. This notion is that same initial impulse that has prompted the publisher to start this *Asian Architects* series in the first place.

While we are generally inclined to flip through architectural publications and their glossy, orchestrated images with alacrity in this age inundated with media images, I suggest that these pages require additional effort on the part of the reader in order to acquire a closer understanding of the complexities involved in the production of architecture in this part of the world. A closer engagement beyond the obvious sleek presentation, could possibly reap greater rewards.

Tan Kok Meng

Several years ago, William S. W. Lim, whom I have known for many years, and his wife, Lena, asked me for my opinion of their project to publish a series of books on contemporary architecture in Asia. Their idea was to be quite selective in the choice of works and, instead of merely explaining and introducing buildings, to clarify the nature and direction of contemporary architecture in Asia through the inclusion in each volume of critical essays by a number of architectural historians and critics now active in the region.

I expressed my enthusiastic support for the project. Intellectual activity, as measured in publications, exhibitions and workshops, has lagged behind economic activity for too long in much of Asia.

Asia is the largest continent in the world, and today the enormous energy of its population and vast pools of investment capital from outside are being funneled into building production. This infusion of energy and capital has helped to improve infrastructure such as housing and to develop both commercial facilities including offices and tourist facilities that take advantage of the scenic beauty of the region.

Nevertheless, few of the buildings being produced under present circumstances are worth a pilgrimage of the kind architects make to note-worthy structures.

Naturally, architects will always be drawn to old ruins and the vestiges of ancient cities. In addition, the superb examples of colonial architecture from the latter half of the nineteenth century to the beginning of the twentieth and the many works of vernacular architecture remaining in various parts of Asia are of intellectual interest to that small number of people who specialise in architecture.

What is missing in the region, it seems to me, is an understanding that the buildings being currently produced and the architectural heritage of the past

Foreword

form, in effect, a single entity that is continually evolving. What is required is a deeper insight into the social, cultural and political dynamics behind this evolving entity.

In many regions of the world today, a collision is taking place between modernisation, which calls itself globalisation, and an old culture. The older and more substantial the culture, the greater is the impact of that collision, and at times the encounter gives rise to an identity crisis. Asia is no exception. Yet the conflict between tradition and contemporaneity or modernity has recurred throughout history and is not unique to our times. The only difference today is the enormous scale of the changes that are taking place and the rapidity with which those changes must be assimilated.

By a deeper insight, I do not mean a profound philosophical inquiry is required. What we need is the sensitivity to understand the various phenomena occurring every day around each one of us in a broader, global and historical context. We must understand ourselves and the society we live in and regulate our actions accordingly as in no previous period. That is, we must discover, in this age of globalisation, similarities in phenomena we thought were different and differences in phenomena we thought were similar. Architecture is one of the most powerful media to express these characteristics.

In a region such as Asia, which is characterised by great diversity of religion, race, language, custom and geography, compared with, say, South America, cross-cultural communication and understanding are vital to the establishment of each cultural identity.

Several years ago, my friend, Sumet Jumsai of Thailand, published an excellent work of research. *Naga: Cultural Origins in Siam and the West Pacific* showed how an abundance of symbols of water and the waterside has existed for several hundred thousand years in a region that encompasses Indonesia, Thailand and Vietnam, as well as China and Japan. It made clear that in no other region do so many such symbols appear in genres of art ranging from literature, dance, folkways and sculpture to architecture and city planning. That book showed us how intellectually exciting it was to explore the region from a cross-cultural point of view and to understand the similarities and differences that exist in the diverse symbols of everyday life within a broad temporal context.

Within Asia, geographical features take on many different aspects, and different cultures have created very different cities and buildings. Nevertheless, to the extent that cities and works of architecture are the spatialisation of the order of human life and the surrounding natural environment, Asian, as opposed to Western, qualities can be said to exist. For instance, the spatialisation of order in Western cities and architecture is based on an aesthetic in which mass is organised into figure and ground, generating a formal order. In Asia, by contrast, natural forms – including water, as Sumet Jumsai points out – actively participate in the creation of order, and the result is an order that is more informal and relaxed in character. The aesthetic focuses, not only on mass, but on the insterstices created between buildings, and this interest in giving those voids meaning is closely related to the concerns of Asian religions. The ideas of *ma* and *oku* in Japanese culture, for example, have much in common with such ways of establishing order. It is only when such a foundation exists that cross-fertilisation becomes the driving force for the creation of a new culture and expression.

Issey Miyake, one of Japan's best known fashion designers, was the first contemporary designer to place more importance on physicality, including functionality, than on decorative quality, and it would not be an exaggeration to say that his creations started a worldwide revolution in clothing. At the moment, he is holding a provocative exhibition at the Cartier Foundation in Paris. The theme of this exhibition, which young French designers are forming

Fumihiko Maki

lines to see, is "making". The focus is on design, not as an end product, but as a process that begins with the initial idea and ends with the realisation of that idea, and this theme is explored through various media including computer graphic images. In an interview, he remarks that he now begins with a single sheet of cloth and with it explores diverse designs. He imagines that single sheet of cloth as, say, an African garment or an Indian sari. Naturally, since he employs only a single sheet of cloth, the material takes on more importance that would a material in a decorative article of clothing.

Listening to him discuss his interest in extreme simplicity, process rather than end result, and material, I marveled at the parallels with architecture. It was an eloquent reminder that a cross-cultural viewpoint opens up new horizons for the imagination. Similar efforts at cross-fertilisation are evident in music and other genres.

I am convinced that this publication will enable us to develop new points of view with respect to the relationship between Asia and the West and cross-cultural activities within Asia.

I have always believed that tradition or cultural identity is not something that is simply imparted to us by the past. Of course the preservation of our heritage is an important responsibility of society, but that in itself will not provide us with the motive force necessary to create the future. Tradition can only help us shape tomorrow if we ourselves are willing to undergo change. The development of tradition needs to be understood as a dynamic process. Architecture in that context must be seen as a device for committing the future to memory.

Working on this series of books on contemporary architecture in Asia has caused me to reflect on my relationship with "Asia", or I should say, the Asias I have known. The significance of the title lies in a hard won belief. We construct our worlds out of the daily actualities of our provinces in dialogue with the best conversation that the metropolis can provide.

As I explain in this essay my life has been the crucible for the forming of this belief. Split between South Africa and England I expounded this idea with increasing urgency in my teaching at the Architectural Association in London in the 1980's. Then I extended the practice of the belief in the context of my appointment to RMIT University and a life further bifurcated between this region and the broader metropolitan discourses of Tokyo and New York. Now I am concerned to replace the old definition of the Metropolis as a dominant city region – a definition that died with New York's final fling with modernism in the 1970's according to Ignasi de Solà-Morales – with this new definition: the world conversation. As former Deputy Prime Minister of Malaysia Anwar Ibrahim writes: "In the realm of (humanist ideas) neither East nor West can lay exclusive claim. The ideas are universal…" (Anwar Ibrahim, *The Asian Renaissance*, Times Books International, Singapore & Kuala Lumpur, 1996, p 28).

Here I suggest that each one of us should, to paraphrase Gaston Bachelard, "speak of their roads and roadside benches: the frothing of the hedges I keep deep within me. Thus we cover the universe with drawings we have lived." The record of those sensibilities should be as important to us as the abstractions of economics that tend to dominate our lives. These are the insights that illuminate the realm of architectural reality. These submerged realities are more complete, more of the universe, more able to connect us with its flows. Respect for such realities is more able to create a caring environment than is fear, even fear of ecological or economic catastrophe.

This essay stems from my concern that these realities should be spelled out. These are the terms of my engagement with this 'wonderful world'. I revel in the accounts made by Goh Kasan and others. These are fragments of contemporary Asia's "Songlines". Sing on sweet world, until I end my song…

Leon van Schaik

Architecture in Asia: Province and Metropolis

The Project of the Province

"Memory doesn't care where it lives," Raymond Carver, quoted by Salman Rushdie in *Imaginary Homelands*.

This essay uses a filmic metaphor that has been developed in collaboration with Peter Lyssiotis, whose images are companions to the text.

Let me declare at once that a book about Architecture in Asia conceived of in Singapore is a view from the edge, a child of a diaspora. I declare this because I know that there is a valency built into our perceptions of the world and I want to acknowledge[1] and enthusiastically embrace that valency. Let me further declare my hand: I am a diasporean before I can claim citizenship of any particular place. I share this experience with the intelligentsia of all of the great displacements created by the now[2] almost deceased colonial project of Europe. Even without the obvious stretching of the geographies[3] of our imaginations that we post colonials are familiar with, the information age is creating multinational connections for all media consumers. For both reasons, all of us have multi-layered identities, the least significant of which are the broad-brush national categories[4].

1 If there is one thing that we have learned from Said, it is that we must acknowledge such valencies. Said, E., *Culture and Imperialism*, Chatto and Windus, London, 1993.
2 (post Hong Kong).
3 Davenport, G., *The Geography of the Imagination*, Pan Books Ltd., London, 1984.
4 Hobsbawm, Eric, Professor of History in London and New York in a Television Documentary series entitled "What My City Taught Me".

Today, I am an Australia based, London educated transnational with a thousand year Anglo-Dutch heritage and an eidetic memory of Africa. One of the tides that tugs on this locus is Asia. I had no idea that Asia would play a part in my life when I was a child in South Africa, or when I was a young man in London. No one is that isolated now. Sure I had a conception of "The East" as a child. My paternal grandparents had a home filled with willow patterned crockery and precious china figurines of mandarins and peasants on every mantelpiece. We moved around these in awe. Piecing it all together now, I realise that the war of cultures between my Anglo and my Dutch heritages was also at a basic level a food war. I now know that the food in that household was Nonya. It was so unlike what we were accustomed to in a domestic realm dominated by my maternal grandparents – where the food swerved between sedate English and hot Indian. I could not plumb the depth of the bitterness in this divide. My Oupa left Holland at the age of nineteen to help the Boers fight the invading British[5]; my Ouma's brother had died in a British prisoner of war camp in Ceylon. They identified viscerally with everyone who lived under colonial subjugation. My Anglo grandparents, on the other hand, listened to the Queen's speech on shortwave wireless at Christmas, and identified with a 'home' thousands of miles away from where they lived.

So it was in Africa that I was imbued with a sense of the depth of Asian civilisation[6] while I was simultaneously inducted into the trappings of belonging to the master-class of British imperialism. For me, as for so many of the client groups of imperialism, be they Tamil or Cantonese, this proved to be a cruel hoax when I began searching for my own identity without the support of that pretend 'home': it was a long way from Kansas[7]. Singaporeans of the next generation – like Goh Kasan[8], for example, are split between tens of thousands of years of Hokkien tradition, a thousand years of Malaysian multiculturalism, London, and the successes of Lee Kuan Yew. We have all grown up through such shifts in the focus of our lives: in my family the Chinese, especially the Nonya, have been a consistently admired group, but the Japanese and the British have shifted in and out of favour dramatically depending on whether their imperial ambitions were battering on our doors.

5   The Anglo-Boer wars were two wars fought in South Africa between the British and the Boers, people mainly of Dutch descent. The first war lasted from 1880 to 1881, the second was fought between 1899 and 1902. They were caused by various attempts by the British to annex the Zuid Afrikaansche Republiek, ultimately in order to control the gold found in the republic. The British introduced many elements of modern warfare: concentration camps being the most evil innovation. 40,000 people died in these camps.
6   So it was in Africa that I was made aware of the tragedy of a shared loss of autonomy and a shared loss of the respect that goes with self-determination. My PhD records my induction into African civilisation.
7   *The Wizard of Oz* documents such a search and its fruitless(?) outcome.
8   Goh Kasan, *H2O and Other Proselyrics*, Landmark Books, Singapore, 1996.

There's a cruel irony in the way that the post colonial generation, not subject to these experiences, is adopting the trappings of USA style as a contingent identity. This is more than Coca-Cola, baseball caps and Nike: it is also the very fabric of our new cities. Airports, Shopping Malls, Corporate Towers and Hotels. Big Mac Cities.

But we must be careful not to nurture a "Volk" architecture of the East. No one should be willing to transfer the colonial burden of "Orientalism" into a new "Asianism". That way, in the proverb of my childhood, lies 'the madness for those whom the gods would destroy', and I certainly won't carry that sort of guilt. I do want to celebrate new fusions in architecture, fusions between our individual actualities – our 'Provinces' – and the global 'Metropolis' that this new century will see emerge fully from the chrysalis of information technology. I declare that the re-assertion of pride in the cultures of the old "Metropolises" of Asia, while not the only factor, is an important consideration in the emergence of a new architecture that is more than a 'mirror of modernity'[9]. It is fruitless to call for the preservation of the cultures of nationalism without acknowledging their inevitable dark sides. Witness the absolute lack of 'fair play' in the British invention of extermination camps during the Boer War. Witness the atrocities of the Japanese war machine in Nanjing, and throughout Asia. We reach surer ground only when we concentrate on the multiple layers of culture embodied in each one of us. We do well when we look to the specific regions of our childhoods, the myths of our families, the food of our ancestors; and then weave the new from the particular intersections of our experience with the best ideas of the global metropolis.

---

9 I argue that individual acts of creation bringing specific actualities into play within the discourse of the world will determine the nature of the Asian 'Renaissance', and its architectural expression.

The Project of the Metropolis

If we do this, the twenty-first century will be the time when cultural colonisation of the world will be overwhelmed by the reverse flows of creativity based on specific experiences; not on nationalist abstractions.

One or Two Things I Know About Her: I use the title of Godard's film about peripheral Paris as the key to these architectural tales of my decade-long encounter with Asian cities. The film was my first encounter with the idea of the 'edge city', the new city of the new world but forged already in and around and between the historic cores of Europe. And now for the jump cut... Airports.

You can get an outline of a country from its Airport. Jan Smuts in Johannesburg was a monument to Apartheid, a traffic system that streamed from international unity into ethnic difference through gates and tunnels: gates and tunnels that resonate with those of the stadiums where political prisoners have been held, from Shanghai, to Santiago. Heathrow in London says a lot about England's 'muddle through' approach to long term thinking. Charles de Gaulle in Paris speaks volumes of Gallic logic and focus. Kingsford Smith in Sydney says everything about Australia's tenuous grip on big ideas (something that Burley Griffin and Utzon learned in a harder way). Long before you reach the city, Bangkok Airport teaches you about the role of the military in its economy, about the intensity of its hybridisation – a message that is then reinforced both by V8 engines on poles powering traditional hulls through the canals and by the distribution of the elements of a cathedral up and down a hotel tower. Bombay Airport used to introduce you to all of India's poverty before releasing you into the glory of its high Victorian institutions, its modernist esplanade. And what message does the total symmetry of Singapore's Changi arrival halls convey? That you are in for a free for all? The very name still causes hearts to miss a beat in fear. Marc Augê is simply wrong. International Hotels may be 'Non Places'. Airports are not[10].

10 Augê, Marc, *Non Places: Introduction to an Anthropology of Supermodernity*, London, Verso, 1996.

The Law of Unintended Consequences

Jump cut to Hong Kong. Hong Kong was the first Asian city to colonise my imagination. It turned my life on its head. Every certainty about the failure of modernism fell subject to doubt when I wandered the upper deck walkways, the high rise emporiums, the high rise housing, the scum of each succeeding wave of waterfront elegance concealed behind the congealing edge of the next land reclamation project. I observed how ancient China welled out of every interstice in the modernist superstructure, completely unimpeded by the new. Sipping strong tea and condensed milk on the now lost municipal pier and staring back at the Peak, dominated by Foster's now over-towered grey colonial battleship bank, I discovered that I was in love. Here was the city of my generation's dreams – alive all the way up. I wandered Kowloon looking for the Air China ticketing agency, where I had to collect my ticket to Nanjing – electronic transfer only went so far then – and found myself wandering the bourgeois elegance of London's St John's Wood. Years earlier, I had listened to my father happily recalling how he had won the Hong Kong Tunnel project for his firm, spent weekends in Harley Street poring over the models and catching a whiff of the excitement this city generated. I loved the thickness of the atmosphere, the palpable space between buildings, the unblinking lights, the bamboo legerdemain of the street scaffolds, the tin trams, the food and the shopping. Two years later I spent some weeks in Hong Kong with Sand Helsel and students from RMIT and the Architectural Association. She had sprained her ankle and we walked slowly through the city locked into close observations. I walked with her through the walled city. She was dressed in a pink linen outfit, fresh from New York. I wore my seersucker Hilton Weiner, and as the song goes, we were "ripe for the picking". We wandered the lanes finding all China wrapped up in this tight parcel. We were based in the Journalists' Club and Hollywood Road was our contour of delight. We fantasised about an escalator from the seafront to the Midlevels. The idea got into the papers, and now exists. It is not as elegant as we imagined it. More elegant than anything we imagined however are the restaurants and bars that line its sides in a glorious metropolitan glissade. Then, in the Times bookshop, I bought "The Swimming Pool Library"[11]. It foreshadowed this future well. On the walkways, I witnessed through acres of yellow chrysanthemums, stock exchange collapses. The *nouvelle pauvre* down to their last Rolls Royces partied away the petty cash at the Mandarin smiling through clenched teeth. And lived to be *riche* again. Anything was possible. At night, looking out from the Star Ferry, I knew this was the most beautiful city on earth. Chasms of artificial valleys open up to the Peak in endless vistas of the

11 Hollinghurst, A., *The Swimming Pool Library*, Penguin Books, London, 1988.

probable; the achingly desirable. And there must be more to come. Despite the monoliths of Foster, Rudolph and the rest, the best of the city is the way in which its walkways are co-opted into the foyers of each new development and out again into the lush tropical air by local architects like Rocco S. K. Yim. Hong Kong! Who cannot love her?

And the most endearing of the one or two things I know about her is that she has not yet found her architectural metier. Witness the pink lumpen mass of the arts complex, the squat crab of the convention centre, the tawdry plush of the hotels. The renaissance is nascent.

Deviance and Care

Cut to Nanjing. In 1987 I flew from Hong Kong to Nanjing in a CAC plane that smelled of the hay it most recently transported, perhaps to Happy Valley. We landed in the dark, in a field lit only by the lights of the aeroplane itself, and taxied for a long time through elephant grass, turning eventually towards a plate glass window surmounted by a red star. We walked down the stairs and across the tarmac into a huge lounge. We sat in china blue sofas while our luggage was consumed momentarily by an antediluvian X-Ray machine. A greeting party welcomed me as the same person whose name they had printed with red ink onto paper attached to the stick they waved. We drove through the night. I remember with stunned fascination what seemed like hours of travel down tree-lined roads. Men in white singlets played billiards by lamp light under Plane trees. Eventually we turned into a compound, and drove between neo-classical piles to International House – a simulacrum of Yorke, Rosenberg and Mardall white-tiled orthodoxy. Here I had a room, home to me for the next two weeks, in which all was a half remembered translation of the West into an unworking symbol for a WC, a shower, hot water, AC. The linen was fresh daily. The breakfast was honey laced through a bread-like substance, the beer strong, the protein banquets a test of endurance. I gave lectures, and in a curtained car, heavily chaperoned, I visited Sun Yat Sen's Memorial. I had been a long haired, bandana'd London trendy who read Mao's Little Red Book, now I was visiting tombs devastated by Red Guards. There was the great bridge across the YangTse, dual carriage ways on which peasants threshed rice and oncoming traffic, turning right, ran towards you in the fast lane before veering off at the last possible moment into the country. We drove down lanes along the banks of canals and I saw images from my grandparents' mantelshelves come alive. Here we visited superb mahogany-panelled hotels, the lake in which Li Po – and every other person who was ever a poet – died drinking to the moon, gardens of intricate rock-work, decks of chrysanthemums, ancient dark wooden chairs. In one town I was introduced to the family in a shop house who firmly believed I was carrying a message from a long lost son in Chicago. I was infatuated with the 'handsome director', the old houses, the temples, the sheer pride and resistance to disaster of it all. One day I ran away from my minders and got hopelessly lost beneath Nanjing's Plane Tree canopy, wandering blissfully for hours until accosted by seriously aggressive currency racketeers. Suddenly the safety of the campus seemed like a good idea. I marvelled at the sheer delight of paper toys, ruined walls, older stones and the extraordinary will to life in a city that had been raped and ransacked again and again. Nanjing will not die[12]. In the

evenings, as all the aeroplanes were commandeered for a Party congress that was to bring in a new guard, I waited out my time watching the proceedings and trying to pick out the word for rain from the weather report. I failed. This word was not included in the one or two things I knew about Nanjing.

Cut to Beijing. Eventually a flight in an un-pressurised plane was made available. We flew for hours at roof top height, a height that enabled us to peep into every peasant household. I saw the wealth of ages in that countryside. Beijing. I remember the ancient feel of the road from the airport. The awful hotel. The awesome wonder of my days in the forbidden city. My walk on the Great Wall, where I soon outstripped my guides and the other tourists and became alone. Here I felt I was an adult for the first time[13]. The first frosts saw the streets lined with cabbages. I feared the ubiquitous presence of the army, and felt the weight of Soweto. This feeling was one of the things I knew about Beijing. So, despite the 'handsome director's' declaration that nothing like the Red Guards would happen again, I was unsurprised by the Tiananmen Square massacre.

Cut to Macau. How out of context that Baroque counter-reformation facade on this isthmus in the South China Sea? How enticing the connections preserved then between sixteenth century Europe and ancient China. Has this all, as it now seems, been overwhelmed by Casino Mafia? Can all those tides of ambition be so easily dispersed? On a circuit of the sea wall, a temple yard exploded with exuberant tails of red jack fireworks making cracks in the lazy afternoon. China and its beliefs poured through every fissure of this environment, a Portuguese meal enfiladed by Cantonese cooking, the villas promising a home that one longed to inhabit but never would, the time gone, the money not yet come... I knew her in a state of suspension.

12 Perhaps the most extraordinary testament to the human spirit I have ever encountered.
13 Having seen this timeless monument to man's creativity – beyond which I was told, countless millions of trees were being planted to halt the advancing desert.

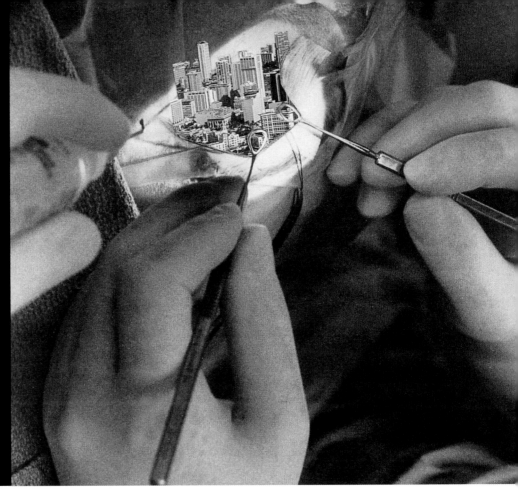

Cut to Kuala Lumpur (KL). On my first visit to KL, I saw a colonial backwater putting on the brave face of modernism. Expatriate architects who were not allowed to do Jane Drew Tropical Architecture at home, did Fry here. Otherwise the grass lined lanes had all the grace of Gandhi's Pietermaritzburg, some of the scunge of Maseru, all of the awful bilingualism of my childhood, the familiar food and the half familiar language of 'Douane', 'Bagasie'... So soon KL became a site for ambitions that put that quiet suburban, late Sunday afternoon dream to sleep for ever, or at least until another day. Now it puts Gustav Dore's London to shame. Against the grain of this unplanned explosion, two generations of professionals with transnational credentials are creating an architectural culture that is a magnet to the bright and the good from all around the globe. Those who manage to ride the wave of development and hang on to the one or two things that they know about her will simultaneously advance the ideals of their architecture. They are a significant minority – a node in the metropolitan discourse far more important than their numbers would suggest. The weave between local actualities and the best thinking from the best academies in the world is making waves, perhaps more potential than real, but waves nonetheless. And you need a wake in order to enter the debate. 'Seen to be heard' is the rule.

Cut to Singapore. Singapore promises much less than Hong Kong, but delivers more. Its Museum-zoo of architects is less well chosen, its site less forgiving, the message of its meticulous gardens does not hint at the sublime in the way that the Peak does. The absence of the public 'dark' in human affairs almost always betokens a hidden problem – Swiss wealth brokered out of holocaust gold. Many have their misgivings about the culture of control on the island. But it is far more complex than that; and like Hong Kong it nurtures an alert intelligentsia. Unlike Hong Kong this finds its expression not in a democracy movement but in the counter culture of its art, architecture and theatre. And here lies a source of energy and of hope. It is too easy to dismiss the decency of Singapore's project, one that provides access for all citizens to the best in transport, housing and services. Architects like William Lim who believe in radical design theorised this evolution out of Fabianism into neo Confucianism. They also built the city in its heady pioneering days, before cargo-cult modernism prevailed. Never mind that politicians misquote Confucius to justify more control than any system could need, as John Ralston Saul[14] has pointed out. It is also too easy to miss the export of the diseconomies of Singapore into the region. But characteristically the most eloquent philosopher of this irony is a Singaporean: Tay Kheng Soon. Most encouraging of all, though, is the way in which Singapore accommodates its past in its present without denial. Benign Orchard Road. Romantic Raffles. Malevolent Changi. She lives her history and this is one of the best things we will know about her. Difficult but familiar. Worrying and stimulating. Prickly and calm. This is a part of the world that carries its history in its food, its elegance on its back and its future in its heart. Knowing these one or two things about her, who could fail to be enthralled?

14 Saul, John Ralston, *The Unconscious Civilization*, Penguin Books, Australia, 1997. Confucian qualities (p 192): arts of peace; of goodness; of superior behaviour which is the opposite of the petty and the mean; of propriety and grace; and finally of the just use of power. He poses the question (p 32): what can humans realistically achieve and sustain for some time? He answers (p 186) "a balanced use of our qualities". His "sensible" list of human qualities is (p 187): "common sense, creativity or imagination, ethics (not morality), intuition or instinct, memory, and finally, reason."

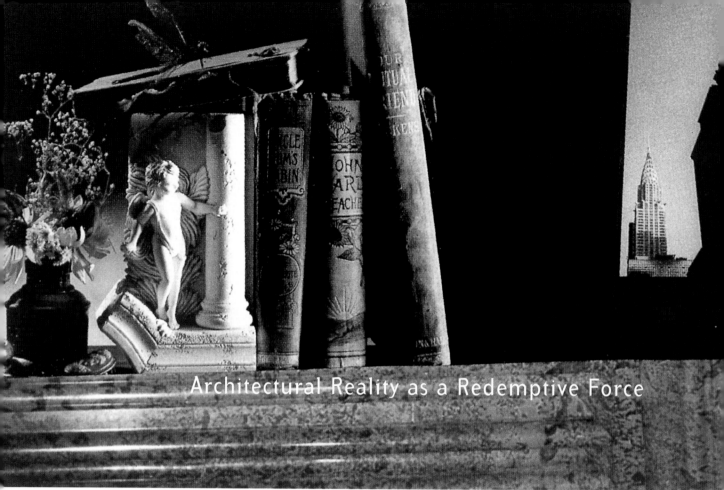

Architectural Reality as a Redemptive Force

Architectural reality matters, if it makes life better. In the metropolis of mind I weave an ongoing fabric out of the inhabitations which engage me. As the engagements deepen, so too does the description that I construct and express in my chosen metropolitan discourses. These are the subjects of my essay in Volume Two (*Asian Architects*). Here I have described the role of these sensibilities. These awarenesses direct us in our duties as caretakers of local architectural cultures. As in the Poetry Club in Cao Xueqin's "Story of the Stone" we must acknowledge the acute formulations of the past, and we must also add our own new insight if we are to contribute to the "Songlines". Whether we innovate or ameliorate, whether we integrate new paradigms or push old ones to new refinements, we do so within a history that is creating 'the ruins of our future'.

All illustrations/images by Peter Lyssiotis.

As I claim in the text: "We do well when we look to the specific regions of our childhoods, the myths of our families, the food of our ancestors; and then weave the new from the particular intersections of our experience with the best ideas of the global metropolis." In doing this we become humble; we acknowledge the construction of others; we celebrate them and begin to care for the physical world, again.

Key to Themes in Illustrations:

The Project of the Province – how the particular achieves resonance with the general; how the eidetic memory (laid down in childhood) fuels Architecture's separate reality (separate from, but inclusive of, the reality of Reason).

The Project of the Metropolis – how the city is the engine of the growth of awareness and therefore of change; how the town (then the city) differentiates us from the nomad, the hunter-gatherer, the feudal; how the city is the locus for 'civil society'; how global protocols nest the cities into a hierarchy of power and responsibility.

The Law of Unintended Consequences – how the growth of a city can also be the engine of our undoing; how we need design that is both local (provincial) and global (metropolitan) in order to deal with this.

Deviance and Care – how scepticism and individual rebellion are the necessary engines of the province, while regimes of planetary care (ethics, politics, economics, love and hope) are the job of the metropolis.

Architectural Reality as a Redemptive Force – how this only exists when we span province and metropolis; connect particular actualities and resistances to the general arguments of world thought.

This work is based on my essays of this title in Middleton, R (ed.) The Idea of the City, The Alvin Boyarsky Memorial Trust and The Architectural Association, London, 1996, pp 156-176, and AA Files: Annals of the Architectural Association School of Architecture #14 Spring 1987, pp 48-53.

evelopers often make more m…
rising land prices than f…
roperty development. Bank…
oth local and foreign, are
…an willing to finance mm…
…redibly large projects. La…
…d property speculation has
…med into an obsession. Too…
…th the stock markets, they
…come legalised casinos wher…
…any fortunes have been ma…
…d too easily. These activit…
…estroy work ethics and dist…
…lues. Greed has become res…
…d has given been given pub…
…cu…tion

William S. W. Lim

Asian New Urbanism and
Social Justice

To some of you, one question may immediately come to mind.

How is urbanism in Asia different from that in the West and what is so new about it?

Asian urbanisation is indeed very different. With exceptions, Asians have consistently rejected the post-war Western planning model. This model includes single usage zoning, high density development in central areas, highway criss-crossing downtowns, and the expansion of suburbia. These planning instruments are now proven to be disruptive and harmful to the environment and quality of urban life. Furthermore, with Asia's different historical and cultural traditions, it is inevitable that its transformation and perceptions of modernity will have its own distinctive Asian characteristics. This must inevitably influence the new directions of Asian urbanism. In the meantime, in response to the intellectual discourse on post-modernism, Western urbanists are now seriously challenging their own accepted planning model and are searching for a new urbanism in response to present values, cultures and lifestyles.

It is in this context that I wish to structure my presentation under four sections. They are:

1 A Global Perspective
2 Tradition and Modernity
3 Asian Urbanism Today and
4 Social Justice

A Global Perspective

In the coming decades, great progress will be made in the sciences. We see a world rid of many diseases. People live longer and healthier lives. Auto designers envisage cars that cannot crash. Teaching will be individualised. At the same time, the rapid introduction of information technology, which led to the creation of the network society, has generated high expectations for a better standard of living and improved quality of life. Unfortunately, this is not to be, as big businesses in the USA supported by the political leadership have successfully controlled and manipulated the new technology and their greatly increased productivity for their own benefit. In the process, companies are able to enforce down-sizing and introduce extensive temporary and part-time employment. Tax rates have been reduced. Welfare budgets are being trimmed down. Internationally, free trade is actively promoted, the money market is rapidly de-regulated, and copyright of intellectual property particularly in sophisticated technology and entertainment industries is being enforced. The rich and the elite are getting richer. The poor are marginalised, and increasingly suffer from social exclusion. Even the large middle class has not really benefited from these years of prosperity.

One of the world's leading social thinkers, Manuel Castells, in his recent trilogy entitled *The Information Age: Economy, Society and Culture* discusses at length what he calls Informational Capitalism – capitalism imposed by the present network society.[1] This network society is ruthlessly efficient. It is flexible, adaptive and innovative. It is totally committed to elitism. It ignores welfare and the economically unproductive. It operates on a borderless space and timeless time. Its prime driving force is money.

At the same time, exploding populations in the developing economies particularly in Asia and Africa present incredible challenges. They call for comprehensive strategies collectively supported by all nations. On the global level, we are still likely to face serious shortage of food grains[2] and to suffer from escalating environmental degradation.[3] However, recent famines in different developing countries are due more to distribution and affordability than global shortage.

It is in this context that the current unexpected economic turbulence particularly in Thailand, Malaysia, Indonesia and South Korea is a timely "wake-up" call for all in Asia. Development analysts and international agencies now claim to have identified the fault-lines in these dynamic emerging economies.

1   Manuel Castells, *The Information Age: Economy, Society and Culture*, Blackwell Publishers, London, 1996/1997. v. 1-3.
2   Lester R. Brown, *Tough Choices – Facing the Challenge of Food Scarcity*, WW Norton & Company, New York, 1996.
3   Lester R. Brown, *State of the World 1997*, WW Norton, London, 1997.

However, many of us see something morally wrong with the austerity programmes presently imposed by the IMF (International Monetary Fund). Foreign banks make reckless loans to Asian banks and companies, and when the loans go bad, the ordinary people have to pay the price. From experiences in Latin America and Mexico, the IMF formula has resulted in declining real wages for years together with substantial increase in unemployment. The poor are made to pay for the excesses of the rich. In poorer economies, the basic needs of food, health and education of the poor are sacrificed. Surely, there must be other ways to resolve the financial crisis, which are more just and equitable.

In the meantime, the highly competitive information capitalism from the United States is forcing Western Europe and Japan to down-size, to de-unionise, to partially discontinue welfare, and in the case of Japan, life-time employment arrangement. Will Western Europe and Japan resist or will they capitulate? The problem is that the present economic model does not have a regulatory element that guarantees social justice and equality. In a recent conference, a Chilean scholar focused his concern on the possible adverse effects of the coming Information Age, which creates a new social class of people who do not have access to information – a new race of underprivileged people.[4] For the less developed countries, the objectives of economic development must include the provision for basic needs and the eradication of poverty. Will the American people wake up and revolt against the present mis-allocation of benefits from technological advancement and higher productivity? Perhaps they will, but only after the illusionary honeymoon with Wall Street's excesses.

4   Sergio Vera M1, "Human Values and Economic Development in the Information Age: Will the benefits of modernity be available to all?" Paper presented at the Symposium: Development and Culture in the International Information Age, organised jointly by the Research Centre for Advanced Science and Technology of the University of Tokyo, the Agency for Cultural Affairs of the Japanese Government and the International House of Japan, February 1998, Tokyo (Unpublished).

Tradition and Modernity

Modernity is seen in the West as the process of historical transformation of Europe and later of the United States. It is based on the Greco-Roman tradition and its subsequent development through the Middle Ages, Renaissance, Reformation and Enlightenment to the Industrial Revolution and beyond. Historically, it was the West that generated and developed the ideas and essence of modernity. Modernity includes the concepts of freedom, human rights and individuality as well as democracy and the rule of law. The West experienced many conflicts in realising its democratic systems. In fact, their wide acceptance was won only after many painful struggles. It is therefore understandable that many in the West have a strong sense of their possession. Western scholars have often divorced non-Western traditions from modernity and classified them as The Other.

During the colonial era, Asian traditions in the ex-colonies were frozen in time. Worse, they were sometimes modified or added to by deliberate intervention in order to satisfy the function, meaning or aesthetic expression of the colonial masters. Let me quote Brenda Yeoh's recent book, *Contesting Space: Power Relations and the Urban Built Environment in Colonial Singapore* : Colonialism does not simply involve political and economic coercion but also ideological and cultural impositions... The colonial encounter often takes on a ritualised form whose maintenance is dependent on the export of notions, systems and practices which displace indigenous forms or re-create them in the image of colonial power.[5]

Many Asian countries are experiencing a protracted step-by-step battle with modernity. With a background of different historical and cultural experiences, Asians have to take a much more painful and disruptive path towards modernity. To integrate the past as a living tradition in today's society is a painful intellectual experience. It can also be socially disruptive and politically sensitive. However, it is an unavoidable process.

Modernisation and economic development are essential for modernity and for effective integration into the contemporary world culture. For the non-Western countries, this is not enough. We will have to re-examine our own past, particularly during the colonial era, in order to correct the many imposed distortions. This is easier said than done.

5 Brenda S. A. Yeoh, *Contesting Space: Power Relations and the Urban Built Environment in Colonial Singapore*, Oxford University Press, Kuala Lumpur, 1996.

Countries with strong cultural traditions had to undergo even century long struggles in order to accept modernity in their own terms. It is therefore not surprising that the transformation to modernity in both China and Japan had to be substantially modified to incorporate the concept of modernity with Chinese or Japanese characteristics. Other countries, especially India and Indonesia, will have to go through similar painful exercises. A Sri Lankan incident provides an excellent example to illustrate the burden of traditions. In 1997, two university students from the lower caste were subjected to severe forms of ragging by their seniors, bringing their lives to a tragic end.[6] In recent months, shops belonging to ethnic Chinese Indonesians were looted and destroyed by mobs to vent their anger and frustration arising from the economic crisis. These countries must be prepared to consciously dispossess their own past and traditions before their re-invention.

Without the heavy burden of the ex-colonial legacies, Japan is clearly the first Asian country to achieve modernity. She is therefore culturally, intellectually and artistically at ease with and actively contributing to the contemporary world culture and intellectual discourse. Japan has led the way to re-code Western dominance, particularly in cultural and aesthetic expressions. In recent years, this has enabled many Asians to achieve international recognition, particularly in the arts, without being considered as The Other.

It is not surprising therefore that leading Japanese architects and artists are now best among equals in the world today, both in theory and design creativity. With adequate financial and human resources, the environmental quality of Japanese cities are improving. They are functioning efficiently, with clear Japanese characteristics which are often incomprehensible to most Western theorists and even Western-oriented Asian scholars. It is in this context that we must examine Japanese urbanism carefully, in the process of formulating new guidelines for the Asian New Urbanism.

6 J.B. Disanayaka, "Culture and Development: The Sri Lanka Experience" – Paper presented at the Symposium: Development and Culture in the International Information Age, organised jointly by the Research Centre for Advanced Science and Technology of the University of Tokyo, the Agency for Cultural Affairs of the Japanese Government and the International House of Japan, February 1998, Tokyo (Unpublished).

Developers often make more money in rising land prices than from property development. Bankers, both local and foreign, are more than willing to finance numerous incredibly large projects. Land and property speculation has turned into an obsession. Together with the stock markets, they become legalised casinos where many fortunes have been made all too easily. These activities destroy work ethics and distort values. Greed has become respectable, and has often been given public recognition.

Asian Urbanism Today

Speed, greed and density are probably accurate descriptions of the rapid development being carried out in major urban centres of emerging economies in the East Asian region. The combination of these factors has created unprecedented conditions that are totally different from the Western experience. Notwithstanding recommendations by numerous Western experts since WWII, few cities in Asia have applied and implemented the post-war Western planning theories, with the exceptions of Chandigarh – an Indian city planned by Le Corbusier in 1949 – and Singapore. It is not surprising therefore that many Western critics are appalled by the disorderly development and chaotic mix-usages in Asian cities. However, Brasilia – the modernist example in Latin America - has been critically described as a repetitious, uniform city marked by huge, efficiently laid-out buildings and separated by vast open spaces and highways. It has reduced the complexity of social life to the brutal simplifications of a blueprint.[7]

It has taken decades for the West to acknowledge that the modernist-based planning theories have many inherent problems, which often result in the creation of boring and sociologically unattractive environment. Some Western scholars, including Robert Venturi and Denise Scott Brown, have only recently discovered the charm and excitement of Tokyo[8], and other Asian centres from Bangkok, Hong Kong to Shanghai. Western understanding of Asian urbanism today is still superficial and incomplete. Perhaps, Asian cities are still able to maintain their attractiveness and dynamism because of their chaotic order, pluralistic richness and unintentional complexity. They can function reasonably well notwithstanding the bad planning, corruption and mis-management, as well as gross under-investment in basic infrastructural facilities.

In Asia, the speed of construction and destruction of the physical environment is incredible. The main reasons are rapid economic development, rapid population growth and concentration of government and investment resources in major urban centres. It was a shock for Rem Koolhaas to discover that much of old Singapore was totally destroyed and re-constructed within such a short period of time. To quote from his book *S,M,L,XL*: "the city (Singapore) represents the ideological production of the past three decades in its pure form, uncontaminated by surviving contextual remnants. It is managed by a regime that has excluded accident and randomness: even its nature is entirely remade. It is pure intention: if there is chaos, it is authored chaos; if it is ugly, it is designed ugliness; if it is absurd, it is willed absurdity"[9].

7 Scott, James C., *Seeing Like a State: How Certain Schemes Improve the Human Condition*, Yale UP, 1998.
8 Robert Venturi and Denise Scott Brown, *Architecture and Decorative Arts*, Institute Publishing Co Ltd, Kajima, 1991.
9 Rem Koolhaas and Bruce Mau, *S,M,L,XL*, 101 Publishers, Rotterdam, 1995.

Asian cities have certainly created unprecedented opportunities to make easy money. Governments in Singapore and Hong Kong generate very substantial revenues from periodic land sales. Cronies of the powers-that-be, too, make their fortunes in land-use conversions. Developers often make more money in rising land prices than from property development. Bankers, both local and foreign, are more than willing to finance numerous incredibly large projects. Land and property speculation has turned into an obsession. Together with the stock markets, they become legalised casinos where many fortunes have been made all too easily. These activities destroy work ethics and distort values. Greed has become respectable, and has often been given public recognition. The recent economic turbulence in the region and the property bubble are closely inter-related. Perhaps, the speculative property boom is a major contributor towards the present regional economic turmoil and instability.

Traditionally, the West creates the dynamics of change and exploration within the intellectual context of rationalism and analytical thinking. In contrast, the East creates an order from the complexity of apparent randomness through intuitive wisdom and holistic approach. Fortunately, the post-modern West and the modernising East has in the last few decades successfully built intellectual bridges for better understanding of each other.

We need to identify the strengths and weaknesses of the present state of Asian urbanism to understand the process of transformation of Asian traditions to modernity, and to examine the critical issues and challenges facing Asian urban centres today.

Weaknesses in Asian cities are increasingly apparent in recent years. Many are badly polluted – from Shanghai to Bombay. Traffic is worsening with Bangkok, Jakarta and Manila at a virtual standstill. Unregulated physical expansion is carried out with minimum supporting services. Destruction of important

historical downtown areas continues unabated, such as the sad destruction of traditional Beijing. Overcrowded squatter areas and slums are expanding rapidly. This reflects the inability of city authorities to cope with massive population explosion.

The millions of urban poor in developing countries are not getting their fair share of economic development benefits. The benefits have been uneven, and the poor are often left out of the race in prosperity. This has resulted in the widening of income disparities. To the poor, they want justice. They want work, they want food and they want land tenure. The big question is: who is really listening to the poor and to their suppressed sobbing and their suffering in quiet despair — who indeed!

In the meantime, many important urban innovations have been introduced. In Hong Kong, extensive second-level pedestrian walkways connect many buildings. They radiate from the central area outwards. The long escalators, like vertical transportation, link central Hong Kong to mid-way. These efficient transport solutions are the result of pragmatic necessity. Both ideas are incredibly innovative. They ensure the central area remains highly efficient, while maintaining the historical road width. This intimacy of urban scale and a walkable central area are definitely attractive features of downtown Hong Kong.

Decades ago, the Singapore government already set out to achieve a realistic and affordable objective, i.e. a green, clean and safe city. In the process, this has improved the quality of life for her citizens and has also produced a positive international image. Sophisticated regulations and high taxes have been introduced to limit the number of cars and restrict car use in central areas during peak hours. Together with a comprehensive and an affordable public transport, Singapore gets well-deserved recognition for her transport efficiency.

Social Justice

World population will continue to grow, and much of the increase will be in the developing economies. According to UN sources, by 2015, nine of the ten largest cities in the world will be in developing countries. The only exception is Tokyo, Japan with 28.7 million. Urban population will double from 2.4 billion in 1995 to 5 billion in 2025, with 80% living in the developing countries. Furthermore, the world's urban population is currently growing 2.5 times faster than the rural population.

Agricultural productivity will continue to increase, but the absorptive capacity for more employment is limited. Massive urbanisation is therefore the only way whereby the world can survive the massive population increase. For the urban poor, cities are symbols of hope – if not for themselves, then for their children. For many, this may just be an illusion. Cities in many less developed countries must manage their limited financial resources more effectively and equitably, particularly the choice of investment in services and infrastructure.

The main cause of urban poverty is low labour earnings and lack of employment opportunities. Because they have only limited skills and education, they end up poor. Job creation is essential to maintain social stability. Pre-mature dis-incentives against labour-intensive goods and methods of production or too rapid rationalisation of industrial production to meet international competitions can greatly increase the problem of joblessness. Child labour, sweat-shop labour or even prostitution provide lots of "degraded" employment. However, this is not a defence for the morally indefensible. The problems are structural and ideological. They cannot be easily corrected by Good Samaritans' sentimentality or the external enforcement of human rights. The economic downturn in some Asian countries has exposed the glaring income disparities just below the veneer of prosperity of the rich and the comfort of the new middle class. Referring to the present Asian economic crisis, Lim Teck-Ghee, a UN adviser said: "The severity of poverty especially in urban areas is so serious and demeaning, you are setting yourself up for socio-economic, if not political, explosion".

The millions of urban poor in developing countries are not getting their fair share of economic development benefits. The benefits have been uneven, and the poor are often left out of the rise in prosperity. This has resulted in the widening of income disparities. To the poor, they want justice. They want work. They want food and they want land tenure. The big question is: who is really listening to the poor and to their suppressed sobbing and their suffering in quiet despair – who indeed!

For the poorer developing countries, provision of minimum housing is still expensive and is often beyond the financial capacity of the authorities. Fortunately, in the warmer climatic region, housing is not the top priority for the urban poor. Their top priorities are land tenure, water supply and garbage collection. The urban poor in many countries such as Thailand and the Philippines have shown considerable willingness to organise themselves to secure and even pay for improved access to water and other basic infrastructural facilities. Land tenure continues to be an explosive issue. It is within the capacity of all governments to make this provision for the urban poor. It is a matter of political will and moral responsibility to do so.

Land is an important resource particularly in major urban centres.[10] Even in free market economies, the government must have the right to control and regulate all developments. The community must be able to benefit from the sale of land, the change of use and increase of development intensity. The revenue generated can be very substantial and should not be lost because of patronage and cronyism.

10 William S. W. Lim, "Land Policies for Urban Development" in *Asian New Urbanism* , Singapore, Select Books, 1998, pp 50-57.

To enhance the environment and quality of urban life, land must be allocated for parks, recreation and other public facilities. Where land is really short and expensive, it must be utilised carefully and effectively. Squatter areas and slums exist because we have not allocated our land resource appropriately. When land is available at affordable prices, people can always construct their own housing and often at high density.

Major urban centres in developing countries with market economies are often provided with disproportional state allocations of human and financial resources at the expense of the rural sector. Furthermore, population growth and increasing affluence have generated demand for rapid physical expansion. This often resulted in the absorption of surrounding fertile agricultural land. This economic dependency and physical expansion are undesirable and unnecessary. The city-states of Singapore and Hong Kong have demonstrated the possibility of operating strictly within the constraint of their own physical boundaries and financial resources. Asian cities should have more autonomy and financial independence as well as be self-sufficient. Physical boundaries should be clearly defined and expansion strictly controlled. This is particularly important in the densely populated, larger emerging economies such as China, India and Indonesia.[11]

Economic development in many emerging economies has certainly brought substantial benefits to the privileged minority, better opportunities for the professional and middle class and even some overall improvements in living standard for the majority. However, the successful application of the free-market instrument does not always ensure the appropriate delivery of basic needs and the equitable distribution of development benefits. Social justice may sometimes be carried out by benevolent rulers, but can only be assured by the empowerment and active participation of the citizenry.

In the less developed countries, it is a social and political imperative that human rights must include economic development rights and basic needs of the poor majority. Asia needs stability to achieve the necessary development goals.[12] However, strong independent civil organisations and active grassroot citizen participation are essential to counter-balance the single-minded and forceful strategies of the developmental states in order to ensure social justice and more equitable distribution of the economic development benefits.

11 William S. W. Lim, "Towards a New Urbanism" in *Asian New Urbanism*, Singapore, Select Books, 1998, pp 92-106.
12 "Jiang calls for action to prevent instability", The Straits Times, Singapore, 25 December 1998.

Conclusion

In Asia, we are now living in a very exciting time. This is particularly the case for the younger generation who will have the opportunity to experience, involve themselves, and contribute towards the rapid transformation that will take place in the next few decades. Our cities are developing at such a tremendous pace – perhaps too fast. But we are all in a great hurry. In fact, we are committed to running such a fast race, we cannot slow down easily. Perhaps, this is the likely scenario that Asian architects and planners will have to deal with. The challenges are formidable. Rapid urbanisation is unavoidable and in densely populated countries, massive rural migration is also inevitable. There will be mistakes – even big mistakes. They are unavoidable. We should learn quickly from them and move on.

In planning cities, we need to provide alternatives, to accept complexity, to encourage irrationality and to foster visual delight. We must develop a multitude of innovative urban instruments. The rapidly developing economies and the rich Asian traditions have greatly increased the complexity of the challenge of change in Asian cities. This process of rapid change is often disruptive and painful. We must be prepared to discard outdated planning theories and practices, and to learn from our collective experiences to develop our own.[13]

The most important function of cities today is to provide the best possible environment and quality of life for everyone who is living and working there. We need parks and recreational facilities. We must actively promote the arts, culture and intellectual discourse as well as active citizen participation and a strong civic society. For the emerging economies, this will be a difficult task. It is impossible to enjoy all the trimmings of consumer luxuries and at the same time to carry out our aspired priorities based on social justice and equity. In allocating resources, hard choices will have to be made between providing golf courses or public parks, luxury housing or housing for the masses and department stores or peoples' markets.

Society is extremely complex and full of contradictions. People are not robots. The needs of each individual are different. Unexpected spaces and unfamiliar forms are exciting. Visual surprises are stimulating. Untidiness, such as that found in traditional downtown areas, is relaxing. Cities need spaces in which people remember, think, experience, contest, struggle, get scared, meet strangers, fall in love, and generally become themselves.

13 William S. W. Lim, *Asian New Urbanism*, Singapore, Select Books, 1998.

With courage and commitment, we can look towards an Asian New Urbanism. However, to achieve our vision, we must be prepared to confront our weaknesses, particularly corruption and cronyism. We must also be prepared to change our mind-set and discard out-dated planning theories and practices. We can look to an urbanism that is people-oriented, pluralistic and tolerant. Our cities must have a bustling street life and endless surprises. They will provide an urban environment that has identifiable Asian characteristics – giving expression to its distinctive cultures, values and lifestyles.

There should be no set rules, priorities or predetermined visual images. Each urban centre is like a living organism, continuously changing and growing at different stages of its development. Our cities must reflect our serious concern for social justice and more accurately their citizens' aspirations, values and lifestyles as well as their nobler visions for more equality, happiness and a better quality of life.

This paper is based on and developed from two of my previous lectures on "Asian New Urbanism", delivered at Design Series Talk, Royal Melbourne Institute of Technology, April 1998 and "Vision Impossible and Social Justice" delivered at "Celebrating Chandigarh: 50 Years of the Idea", Chandigarh, India, January 1999.

Sumet Jumsai ___

Memories of the Future

When I was
a child I thought
as a child ;
but when I grew
up I still thought
-- as a child !

hat probably sums up my oeuvres – in painting and in architecture. In painting, it is exemplified by the self-portrait series called "Me" beginning from 1967 when I was still student to the canvases of the 90s. The series might demonstrate some structural instinct and some sort of progression, perhaps in sophistication; but it also shows child-like reflexes and a constant whim to return to the beginning, the embryo. In "Me 5", big feet and hands are flung in all directions as if, in the Nietzchean spirit, to protest birth.

t could also be an inadvertent reference to Picasso and Le Corbusier whose similar obsession with the limbs, in turn, ink them, so I have been told, to Michelangelo. So apparently have I been told that this is the psyche of sculptors, eople with the penchant to create plastically and hence to subjugate everything they touch, including architecture, o exaggerated plasticity.

bove: "Me 5", Sumet Jumsai 1996, oil on canvas 61cm x 76cm   Top right: Le Corbusier's Monument of the Hand in Chandigarh *(courtesy of Helen Grant Ross)*
pposite page: "Me" (self-portrait) 1967, ink on paper 23.3cm x 32cm

In parallel with the "Me" series, my first architectural scheme, the Silpa Bhirasi Art Centre, Bangkok 1966 (unbuilt) was shamelessly Corbusian. This led quite usefully to periods of sculptural simplification: the "Circular Period" of 1968-73 in which tubular volumes and primary colours predominate, and the "Triangular Period" of 1973-80 in which triangles form the principal composition and the core of spatial exploration. After that I took leave, intermittently at least, of L-C, and immersed myself in robotic imageries while trying at the same time to humanise the machine by exorcising it. In the end, I returned to the primeval toy, a sort of simplified de Chirico-esque planks and planes in

different colours which can be assembled in a variety of ways. It was all absolutely childish, but refreshing. Here we are talking about form as something finite and apparently nonchalant to its environmental context, an absolute anathema to the spirit of the *fin de siècle*. The younger generation of architects would abhor by what I do, namely to purvey finite objects, finite in the sense that they can be placed and displaced almost anywhere without context, like a lunar module, or paintings which can be hung anywhere. Peter Eisenman says he squeezes out of the earth, the geocontext, the essence which dictates his design solutions. He gives this process in design, which only he is capable of doing, some sort of Greek or Latin name which I have forgotten, but which has baffled and hence excited architectural students world-wide. But in reality he is another maker of objects and a very good one at that. Frank O'Gehry is another. Both are absolutely superlative as far as purveyors of objects are concerned. I happen to have been commissioned to do a United Nations-related building for the new international zone at the Place des Nations in Geneva, together with Eisenman, Fuksas, Koolhaas, Perrault and others (who were each given a building to design), although I do not think that anyone is allowed to build anything of worth there, considering the earlier aborted design by L-C.* At any rate, Peter's building is a re-adaptation of his Rome's 21st Century Chapel competition design. The crux of the matter is that if the latter "grew" out of the Roman soil, it could not, surely, have also grown out of the Calvinist terrain. But it did – and it did so beautifully! Transposition of objects is what I preach and practise. This is possibly boring in contrast to preaching and practising going their separate ways. Of course, transposing objects should not mean ignoring the physical and social milieux involved. Appropriate responses have to be made to such constraints and many others besides: structural, urbanistic, economic, political, etc. However, they should not be an end in themselves, although they have to be a second nature to an architect of any worth. It is like the alphabet and grammar to a poet. This brings me to my project in Geneva, the Institut Universitaire des Hautes Etudes Internationales (IUHEI) with its obvious antecedent in the Nation Building and, via the latter through some

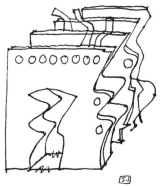

anthropomorphic metamorphosis, in the Robot Building and the Robot Painting. At the time of the Nation Building, I made a reference with reverence to Braque and de Chirico, with a swipe at the Deconstructivists whom I regarded merely as autistic neo-Cubists. Where do we, the 60s generation, go on from here? And what is this *fin de siècle* generation all about? Confronted by the latter, I ask whether we can continue to contribute by being ever in the forefront of any

*The Place des Nations project, as designed by the said group of international architects, was finally stopped by the citizens of Geneva in a referendum in June 1998

philosophy. Specifically, I asked myself whether I should not simply become hermetic. To contribute usefully to society, for example by helping to resolve explosive urban and environmental issues, or by giving a new expression, perhaps even suggesting, a new paradigm to civilisation, in itself presupposes a moral privilege, a sort of residual "Esprit Nouveau" to which so many of us have been subjected, and which inevitably led the more energetic among us to adopt an apocalyptic stand, to see things in terms of crises, or a vital turning point, or the dawn of some neo-Wagnerian world.

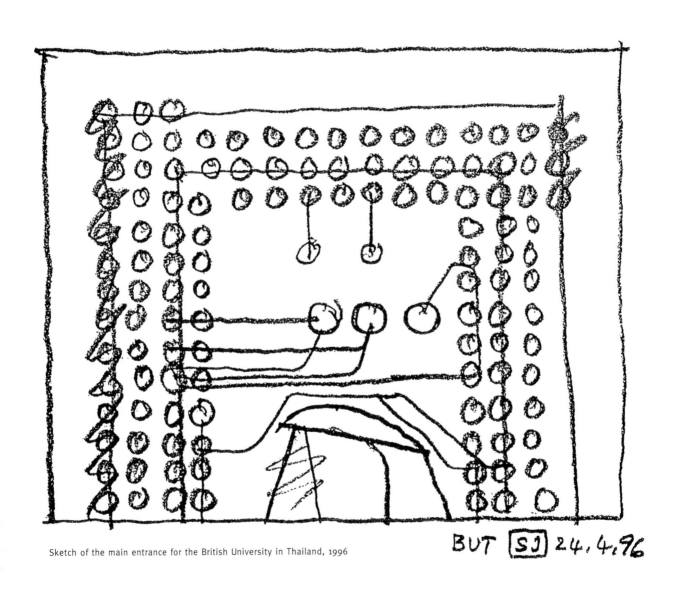

Sketch of the main entrance for the British University in Thailand, 1996

BUT [SJ] 24.4.96

In short, to embrace a sort of architectural eschatology. Inevitably some sort of new Age will occur, and occur it will as part and parcel of the Shivaite cycle so that things are deconstructed in order to be reconstructed, all happening without any millennial upheaval. The new generation, as Shivaite agents, will make a clean sweep of what is left of the forms and objects as they were known and felt by the 60s generation. The 21st century will come out at the other end of the worm-hole with objects of its own, possibly more ethereal, more to do with the mind (or, at the other extreme end, mindlessness) than material, with events no more real or meaningful than digital imaging, and with structural design not necessarily computed on our g-value. Our best behaviour at this point in time is to be a facilitator of the regeneration process. As makers of objects in this century, our object surely is to create memories for the next, and the more child-like, that is, the closer to the process of regeneration, the better.

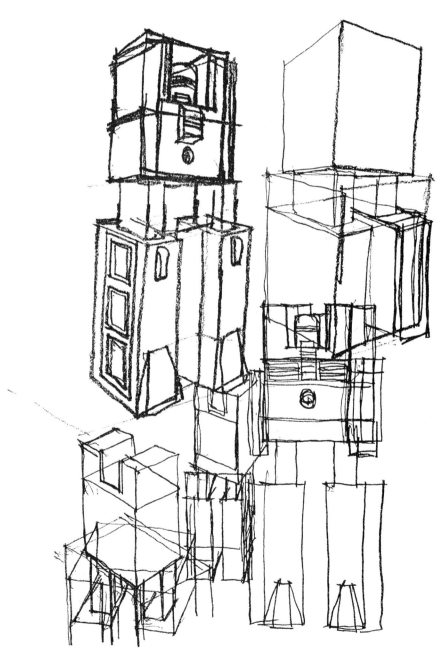

Sketch studies for a second Robot Building, 1985

Opposite: Robot painting 1987, oil on canvas 75 x 9

SUMET
29.12.87

Place des Nations Competition
Geneva. Switzerland. 1995.

Project for new buildings for the UN related international organisation in Geneva.

Design Team: 1995   Sumet Jumsai
                            Thana Chirapiwat
                            Kwanchai Laksanakorn
                            Ekasidh Charoensilp
                            Wolfgang Ungerer
        1996-97   Somjet Rattanapan
                            Helen Grant Ross
                            Stefan Schlau and SJA+3D staff

Local Associates: De Planta & Portier, Architectes, Geneva

In December 1994, the Public Works Department of Geneva launched a programme to build a group of new UN buildings and facilities in Geneva's International Zone in conjunction with a traffic and urban planning proposal for this area. Seven buildings were designated for this area: House for Human Rights and Humanitarian Issues, Universal House to accommodate 45 missions for developing countries, Institute of Strategic Studies (IGCSP), Institute for Political Sciences (IUHEI) and its Library, Place of Worship, and the rebuilding of an international school (Sismondi College). Two more programmes, the World Trade Organisation (WTO) and Interparliamentary Union (IPU), were combined in one building in an adjacent site. The total floor area for the entire project was 61,000 square metres.

The programme was finalised in February 1995 and fourteen architects (seven Swiss and seven international) were invited to submit conceptual designs. A jury which comprised UN ambassadors, experts and eminent architects commissioned Massimiliano Fuksas to conceive the master plan while amongst other international architects, Sumet Jumsai was commissioned with the design of the academic Institute for Political Sciences (IUHEI).

Place des Nations site layout

Competition model

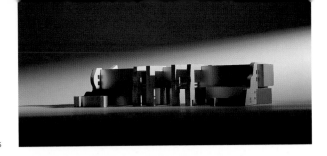

House for Human Rights & Humanitarian Issues

Universal House or Embassies Building

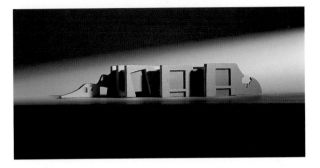

Institute of Strategic Studies (IGCSP)

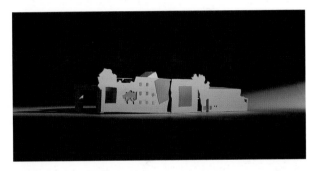

Place of Worship

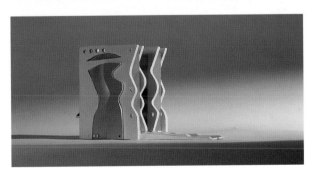

WTO/IPU Building

Concept sketch for IUHEI Building

IUHEI Building

Geneva, Switzerland, 1995.

Fuksas' master plan is based on placing the central group of buildings in a large reflecting pool. IUHEI Building is designed to reflect and enhance this aquatic environment like a piece of sculpture floating on water. The sculptural concept itself is based on the early Cubism of Braque and Picasso with the everchanging planes seen on the elevation from different views. Four "giant wings" or walls, pierced in places, are placed apart forming three parallel bays. The other two sides, facing east and west are glazed walls to receive sunlight, while the central bay also has a glass roof. In winter the heat would be trapped in this central bay; but in summer, it would allow cool air to be drawn across the surface of the surrounding water body into the interior up the central bay through roof hatches resulting in "natural air-conditioning". Water from the basin continues right into the building's central space which is also the main circulation zone with a central staircase and walkway "bridges" linking the two side wings in a seemingly haphazard manner. The ground floor of these two wings is taken up by a student lounge, reception and registration offices and a large lecture room. The basement contains a larger lecture room for 400 persons, an exhibition space and a bar. The upper floors house more lecture rooms, offices, and research cubicles, which are dispersed so that there is a greater possibility for interaction between professors and research students.

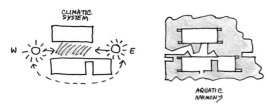

Concept sketches of IUHEI Building

Fifth storey plan

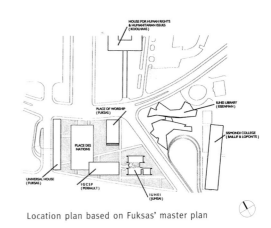

Location plan based on Fuksas' master plan

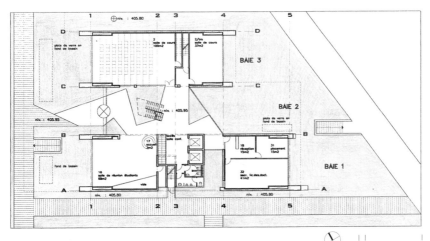

First storey plan

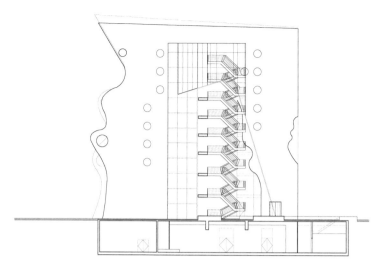

E-W section through Bay 2, looking south

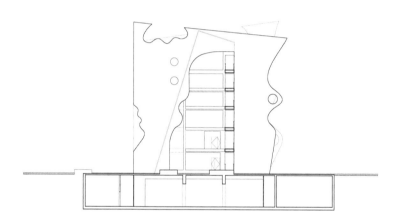

E-W section through Bay 2, looking north

Left: Interior of Bay 2 (hallway), looking up   Right: Computer model of south elevation

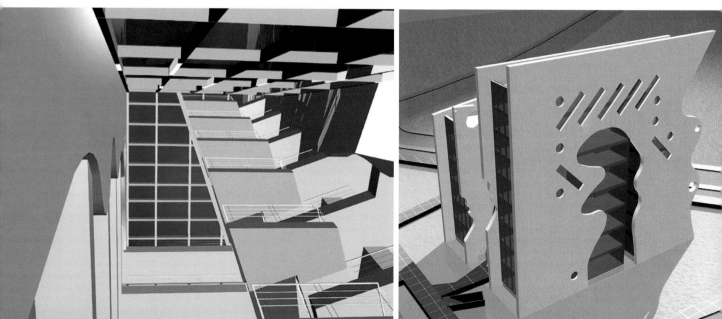

Kansai-kan or National Diet Library Competition

(in association with Stefan Schlau)
Tokyo. Japan. 1996.

The proposed scheme for the new Kansai-kan or National Diet Library is a "prepared landscape". Thin masonry slabs containing all the stacks form lines in a landscape of water terraces, symbolising the dynamic dualism of man-made structure and nature, of acquired knowledge contained in scripts and the spirit of the earth, like the "Rosetta" stones in paddy-fields. This theme of "lines in the landscape" continues throughout the scheme: the generously dimensioned Reading Room is conceived as a light and airy internal landscape in which the lines of reading tables and shelves create a series of open fluid spaces overlooking the water terraces. The Library is seen not as an institutional "building" but rather as a living "land art", blending in naturally in horizontal and vertical layers into the existing terrain. Besides the lines in the landscape, there is another line, very thin, which wraps around the stone slabs in order to emphasise its unity. This line is the line of light that will light up the complex.

LINES (SLABS) IN THE LANDSCAPE

SLABS BLENDING
INTO LANDSCAPE
OF RICE (WATER) TERRACES
(ELEVATION)

THE SCRIPT
= ROSETTA STONES
OR FLOATING SLABS
IN SPACE ODYSEY

Front view of massing model

ITSU KUSHIMA

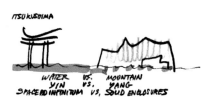

WATER   VS.   MOUNTAIN
YIN   VS.   YANG
SPACE AD INFINITUM   VS,   SOLID ENCLOSURES

LINE WRAPPING
AROUND THE SCATTERED
SLABS (ELEVATION)

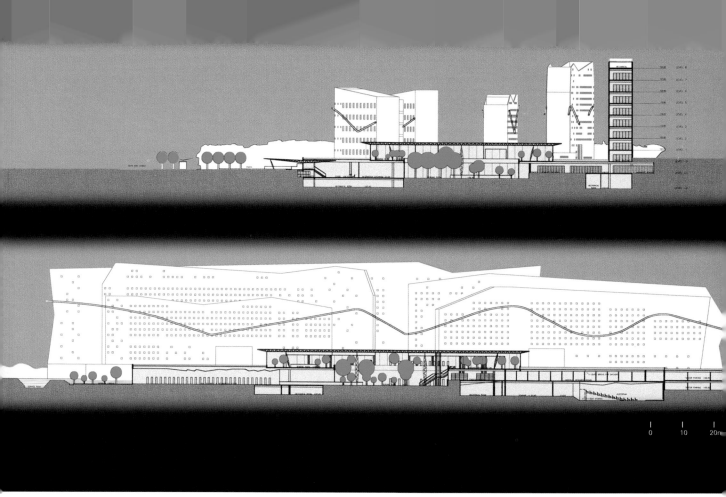

Top: Cross section A-A   Bottom: Longitudinal section B-B

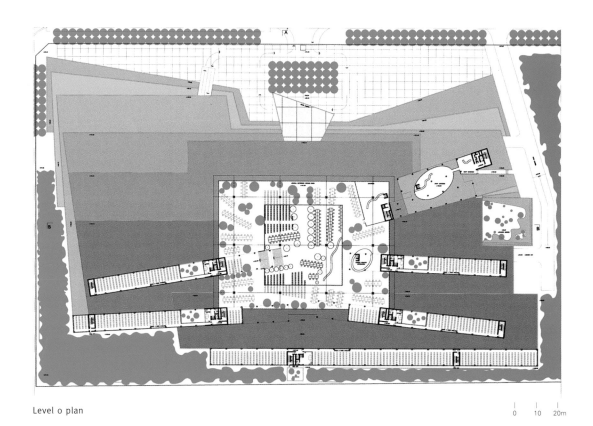

Level 0 plan

0   10   20m

Top: West elevation   Bottom: Northwest view

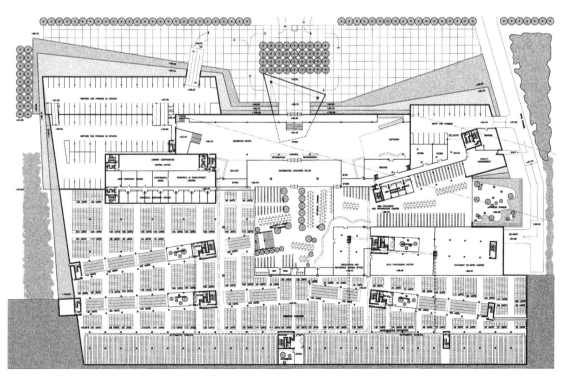

Levels 1 and 2 plan

0   10   20m

The Nation Building
Bangkok. Thailand. 1991.

(Head office of the Nation Multimedia Group, Bangkok)

Located in the southeast suburb of Bangkok on the highway towards the town of Pattaya, the site borders a strip which is undergoing rapid transformation from a rural to an urban environment. Presently, the area has no unified urban texture and probably will not have any later, given the "free-for-all" phenomenon of development which is taking place there. The site, which is approximately 3.6 acres, has a road frontage of 100 metres and a canal running along to one side. Until recently the entire area was a rice field.

The building consists of eleven floors which recedes towards the top. A large triangular frame in reinforced concrete is mounted on top of the roof. Two sides of the frame, slanting out towards the highway, are hollowed to become spaces for electronic panels with running messages giving headlines, weather situation and other information associated with the press. The overall form is like a "head" with cut-outs for "eyes" that peer over the road below.

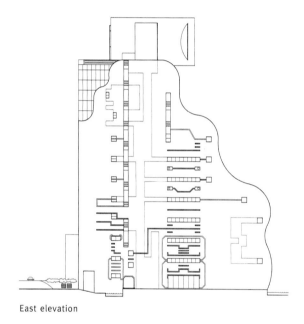

East elevation

Below: West-side view   Opposite: East-side view

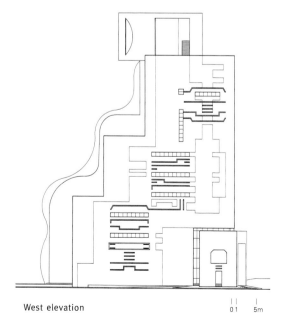

West elevation

0 1   5m

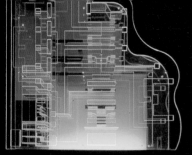

Plexiglass models (above and far right) made
for the Venice Biennale 1996

Sixth storey plan

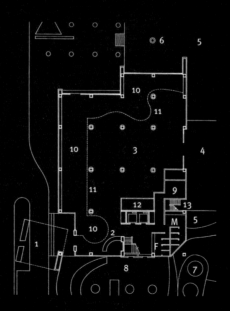

First storey plan

1 Carpark
2 Reception desk
3 Editorial office
4 Lawned terrace in the pond
5 Lotus pond
6 Fountains
7 Condensing units
8 Landscaped mound over
   main machine room
9 Telecom room
10 Double height
11 Mezzanine
12 Machine room (airconditioning)
13 Fire staircase
14 Offices
15 Lawned terraces

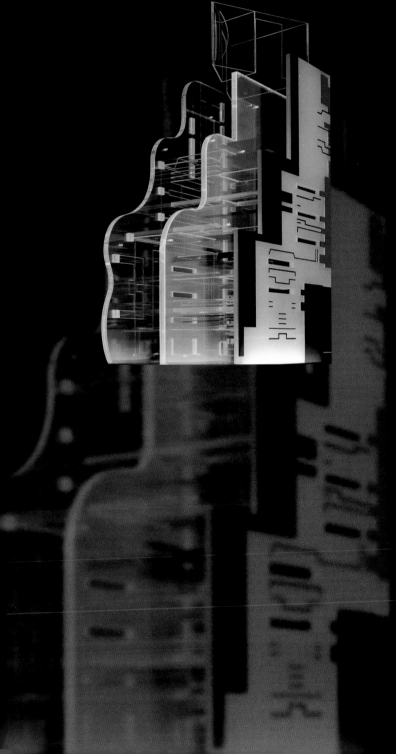

The challenge here was to come up with a design which would sit well in the rice field for a few years, and then afterwards in a "jungle" of non-descript buildings. Besides this there was no other discernible challenge. Even the corporate image was not a prerequisite (if that can be called a challenge!). The site, in brief, is a non-context.

The project began with a painting. A painting that can be carried about and hung in different environments without having to be in context with them. Other fleeting thoughts came at this point: the profile of the chief editor working on a word processor, or perhaps a graphic artist working on a page layout, sitting on a stool; electronic circuitries surfacing here and there; an anthropomorphic remnant of a previous "robotic" scheme (see *A+U* Architecture + Urbanism February 1985 and April 1987); and a Cubist-like painting.
In fact, the influence of Cubism emerged in more than one aspect in the project. The first, a more conventional one, is discernible in the three vertical planes or party walls which, running east-west, starts with a square and rectangular composition and continues to become partly curvilinear, eventually freeing up completely into a free play of curves.
Le Corbusier's late Cubist painting – a sort of simplified Braque, comes to mind here. The second aspect transcends mere physical metamorphosis: Cubism in this case is seen as a collage of the different stages of thought, the design process itself.

Since this is a "painting" that is going to be built, questions about its architectural premise cannot be avoided. The first question must be: Can architecture be something personal and disconnected from the prevailing comprehension about architecture, and if so, would it not lead to a kind of hermeticism?
At this point one may be reminded of Corbusier's chapel at Ronchamp which contains, but puts aside functional, social and even intellectual issues to become highly involuted, personal and spiritual.

Sumet Jumsai

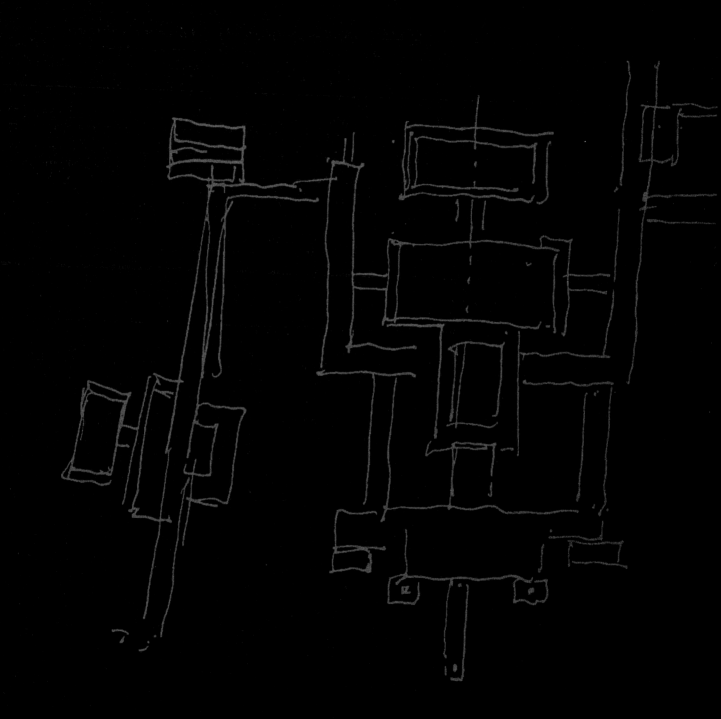

Wu Liangyong

An Architect for the People

Born in Nanjing (Nanking), China, in 1922, Professor Wu Liangyong is one of the distinguished pioneers in urban planning and architecture in China, most noted for his search for approaches towards **a blending of the old and new based on the Chinese spirit.**

In 1946, together with the late Professor Liang Sicheng (Liang Ssu-ch'eng), the doyen of Chinese architectural historians, Professor Wu founded the Department of Architecture in Tsinghua University, and subsequently headed the City and Town Group in the Department. In 1951 he set up the first landscape architecture programme in China, which has grown into the present School of Architecture with 85 teaching staff, 418 undergraduates, 109 master's degree candidates and 41 doctoral degree candidates. He is credited for this growth through his outstanding deputy deanship from the period 1951 to 1966, and his deanship from 1978-1984. In 1984 he set up the first research institute of architectural and urban studies in Tsinghua University, which over the past decade, has made significant contributions in national and international research projects, as well as in training postgraduate students.

Professor Wu has made remarkable contributions in the history of urban development in China and in comparative studies of Chinese, Western and East European planning from a theoretical perspective[1]. He is accomplished in studies on urban culture[2], conservation of historic cities and architecture, and on urban aesthetics[3]. For him **conservation signifies cultural self-respect and consciousness of one's own cultural tradition,** without which it would be hard to express the cultural identity of a Chinese[4]. As a member of the National Historical Conservation Committee of the Ministry of Culture, he is among the strongest advocators for the preservation of historic relics and natural ecology in China[5].

Professor Wu's comprehensive knowledge of the history of Chinese cities and world-wide progress in the field have enabled him to explore in great depth the problems of urbanisation and the possible solutions in China. This is particularly embodied in his regional perspective of urbanisation. He has the view that issues of development may only be resolved through dealing with the associated geographical areas as a "regional complex", rather than individual administrative entities within them. He is credited with the original proposals for the strategic state policies of "development of a co-ordinated system of large, medium-sized and small cities"[6], and "differentiation in developing strategies for coastal and inland areas based on regional differences"[7], which the Chinese government authorities have gradually adopted.

In dealing with urban issues, Professor Wu has been actively promoting a trans-disciplinary approach and his practical research has been a synthesis of regional spatial studies on the urban system, master planning of cities, capital development and infrastructure provision. This has been the research guideline at the Institute of Architectural and Urban Studies for many years. In 1995, upon his proposal, a multi-disciplinary research entity – the Centre for Human Settlements – was set up in Tsinghua University to co-ordinate the research activities in architecture, civil engineering, environmental sciences and management studies and he became the director of the Centre.

Particularly remarkable are his theory and practice in linking architecture and the city, architecture and landscape architecture, and in expanding the vista of architecture in the urban and regional dimensions. Through his studies on urban structure and form, he has identified different growth patterns and models such as the "multi-centre co-ordination model" for Beijing[8], "hill-river-town pattern" for Guilin[9], the "round-sea city" for Xiamen[10], the "round-island belt" for the Hainan Region[11], and various other models for the development of urban structures in historic cities[12].

In addition to his theoretical contribution, Professor Wu has achieved marked success in practical work, which has enabled him to develop and test his theory and ideas. In the early 1950s, he proposed that it was just as important for medical schools to have teaching hospitals, as schools of architecture to have associated design institutes. In 1958, an Associated Design Institute was set up in Tsinghua University, which has grown into a well-established National Class 'A' office with 140 staff and in which he has been the chief consultant architect. As he believes that strategic planning decisions have to be transformed into amenable physical space through good urban design, he regards urban design concept and urban design practice as the fundamental task for architects in China consistent with the trans-disciplinary research methodology. He pioneered the implementation of zoning guidelines to replace the traditional Soviet-type detailed planning. He and his team experimented with a new building type for the historic areas in Chinese cities which is characterised by the low rise, horizontal silhouette, and the human scale. The earlier works under his leadership were presented as part of the Historic Conservation and City Planning Conference and Exhibition in London in 1987.

In the course of his professional practice since the 1950s, Professor Wu has led and taken part in many projects of urban planning and urban design and he has also personally designed a series of important public buildings of symbolic significance, among which are the Planning and Design of the Enlargement of Tian An Men Square[13], the Planning and Design of the National Library in Beijing[14], the Urban Design Plan for Conservation of the Central Area of Guilin, and the New Courtyard House Complex Development at Ju'er Hutong in Beijing. Recent projects that are under construction include the Campus Planning and Design of the Central Academy of Fine Arts in Beijing, the Planning and Design of the Research Institute of Confucius in Qufu, and the Regional Conservation Plan of Northwestern Yunnan. His prototype design of the new courtyard house at the Ju'er Hutong was in keeping with the integrity of traditional urban texture, the neighbourhood structure and the visual harmony in Beijing and has become an outstanding example in conservation of historic areas in China. It received the Gold Medal for Architecture of ARCASIA (Asian Architects of Regional Council) in 1992 and the UN World Habitat Award from the President of the General Assembly of the United Nations in 1993 for this successful design.

For his contribution in academic fields, Professor Wu was elected Member of the Chinese Academy of Sciences in 1981. He was named Honorary Fellow of the American Institute of Architects (AIA) in 1990 for his contributions as "one of the pioneers of architecture and urban planning in modern China, a distinguished educator, a renowned water-colourist, and a prolific author." He is also Honorary Member of the Architectural Institute of Japan. Recently, he received another Honorary Fellow from the Royal Institute of British Architects (1998).

Professor Wu firmly believes in being an architect of the people, for him urban planning and architecture are to bring real benefit to the people and society. At the age of 77, he is as active and energetic as ever at the frontiers of architecture and planning, playing a significant part in teaching as well as in national development policy-making, even fieldwork. For his great contribution to architectural education, he was justly awarded the Jean Tschumi Prize by the UIA in 1996.

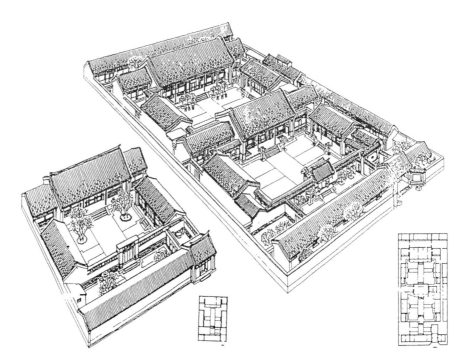

1   See for instance, Wu Liangyong's manuscript, "A Brief History of Ancient Chinese City Planning" (Kassel: Gesamthochschulbibliothek, 1986).
2   Wu Liangyong (1986). "On Urban Culture", Chongqing Urban Studies, Special Issue for the Founding of Chongqing Society for Urban Studies.
3   For instance, Wu Liangyong (1987), "On Urban Aesthetics", ibid., pp 559-604. This is also the title for his forthcoming book.
4   Wu Liangyong, "Toward a Theory of Regional Reality". A keynote speech delivered on the Symposium on "Asian Cities and Architecture in Transition", 1989; Habitat International Vol. 15, pp 3-9, 1991. London.
5   Professor Wu has been the Vice Chairman of the State Historic Preservation Committee. See Beijing Review, June 30th, 1980.
6   Wu Liangyong. "Urban Development Planned on Actual Local Conditions", and "Some Thoughts on Strategic Aspects of China's Urban and Rural Construction". Selected Essays on Urban Planning and Design. pp 74-99 and pp 100-128 respectively. 1987.
7   Ibid.
8   Wu Liangyong. "Proposals for the Planning of Beijing", Architectural Journal. No. 5, 1980.
9   Wu Liangyong et al (1987). Detailed Planning for Guilin's Central Area. Institute of Architectural and Urban Studies, Tsinghua University, Beijing. 1987; "Guilin: Its Present and Prospect—A Search for Urban Pattern and Design Criteria". CEPR-WP06-89, University of California at Berkeley, CA, U.S.A.
10 Wu Liangyong (1987). "Xiamen (Amoy) Special Economic Zone—A General Survey and Planning Proposal". Ibid., pp 179-200.
11 Wu Liangyong (1987). "A Proposal for the Urban Development in Hainan Island". Seminar on Hainan's Planning. November, 1988; "On Urban Conurbation: China's Integrated Coastal Urban Development". Conference paper, 1988, Tokyo.
12 Wu Liangyong (1987). "Restructuring the Historic Cultural Cities—Old Cities Rehabilitation and Urban Design". CEPR-WP06-89, pp 289-309. University of California at Berkeley, CA, USA.
13 Wu Liangyong (1987). "Planning and Design of the Tian An Men Square". Ibid., pp 410-455.
14 Wu Liangyong (1986). "Two Attempts for Architecture of Modern and Chinese".

New Model for Integrated Rehabilitation of Courtyard Houses
Ju'er Hutong
Beijing, China, 1987-1992

The project is located in one of the typical traditional single-storey courtyard housing areas in the inner city of Beijing where urban conservation and housing problems are critical.

In 1987, the first phase of the project had one of the worst courtyard compounds, No. 41 Ju'er Hutong, to test a new housing type in the area aiming to incorporate conservation and renewal. The first phase of the project succeeded in providing 2,760 square metres of new housing, doubling the previous ones on the same site. It greatly improved the housing conditions of the existing residents. At the same time the courtyard way of living was not disrupted.

The second phase of the project extended the success of the first phase to its neighbouring communities,

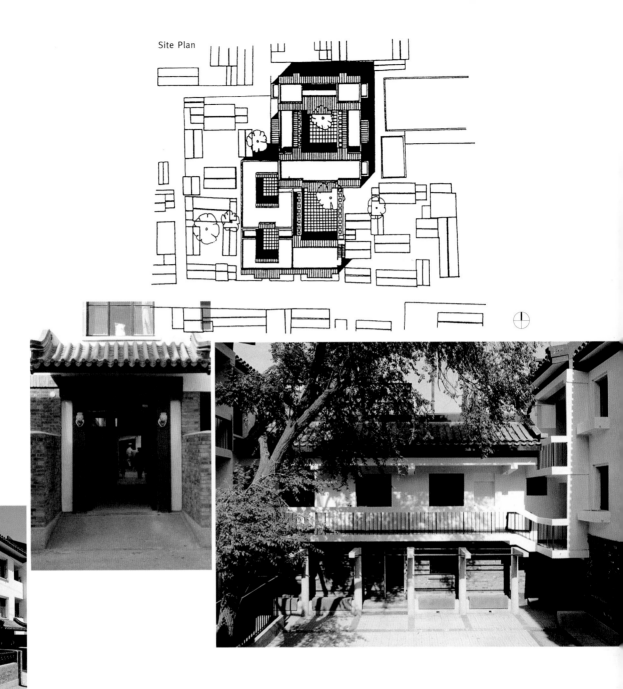

Site Plan

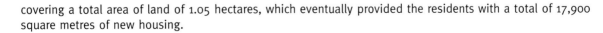

covering a total area of land of 1.05 hectares, which eventually provided the residents with a total of 17,900 square metres of new housing.

The success of the Ju'er Hutong project has drawn great attention both in China and abroad. It has won several important professional prizes including the China Architects' Society Award 1992; the Beijing Special Housing Design Award 1993; The Most Popular Architecture in Beijing, 1994; the ARCASIA Architectural Excellence 1992; and the World Habitat Award, 1992.

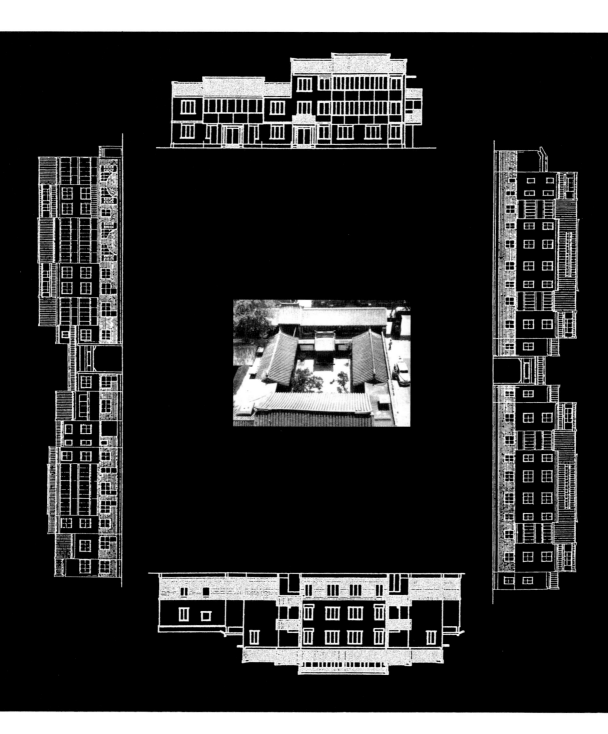

"Beijing 2000" – Urban Design Plan, Shichahai District

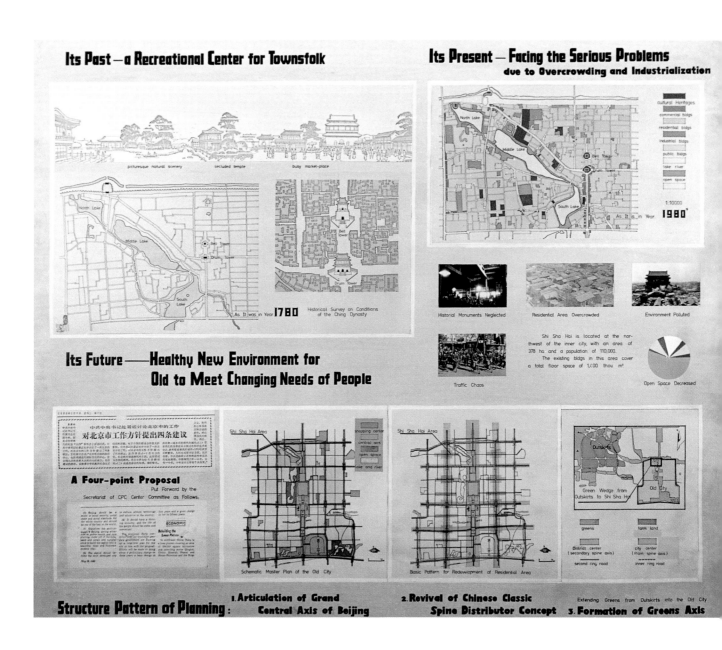

Its Past—a Recreational Center for Townsfolk

picturesque natural scenery · secluded temple · busy market-place

North Lake · Middle Lake · Bell Tower · Drum Tower · South Lake

As It was in Year **1780**

Historical Survey on Conditions of the Ching Dynasty

Its Present — Facing the Serious Problems
due to Overcrowding and Industrialization

cultural Heritages
commercial bldgs
residential bldgs
industrial bldgs
public bldgs
lake river
open space

North Lake · Middle Lake · Bell Tower · South Lake

1:10000

As It is in Year **1980**

Historial Monuments Neglected · Residential Area Overcrowded · Environment Polluted

Shi Sha Hai is located at the northwest of the inner city, with an area of 378 ha and a population of 110,000. The existing bldgs in this area cover a total floor space of 1,00 thou m²

Traffic Chaos · Open Space Decreased

Its Future——Healthy New Environment for
Old to Meet Changing Needs of People

对北京市工作方针提出四条建议

A Four-point Proposal
Put Forward by the
Secretariat of CPC Center Committee as Follows.

ECONOMIC

Rebuilding the Lowe Plateau

Shi Sha Hai Area · shopping center · central axis · open space · lake and river

Schematic Master Plan of the Old City

Shi Sha Hai Area

Basic Pattern for Redevelopment of Residential Area

Outskirts · Green Wedge from Outskirts to Shi Sha Hai · Old City

greens · farm land

District center (secondary spine axis) · city center (main spine axis)

second ring road · inner ring road

Structure Pattern of Planning : **1. Articulation of Grand Central Axis of Beijing** **2. Revival of Chinese Classic Spine Distributor Concept** Extending Greens from Outskirts into the Old City **3. Formation of Greens Axis**

The proposed redevelopment area lies to the west of the grand axis of the Imperial City terminating at two magnificent structures, the Bell Tower and the Drum Tower, like giant sentinels guarding the rear of the palace. Since its founding in the early Yuan Dynasty (13th century) this district has been popular with city dwellers who flock here in search of quietude.

As the name, Shichahai, implies, this district is characterised by a string of three lakes like a necklace set in idyllic greenery punctuated with ancient monuments and princely mansions of old. Because of its location in the rear of the Imperial Palace, Shichahai was designated as a place for trade so that the sight of worldly gains would not distract the Celestial Emperor. This was actually one of the directives for the ancient Chinese town planning.

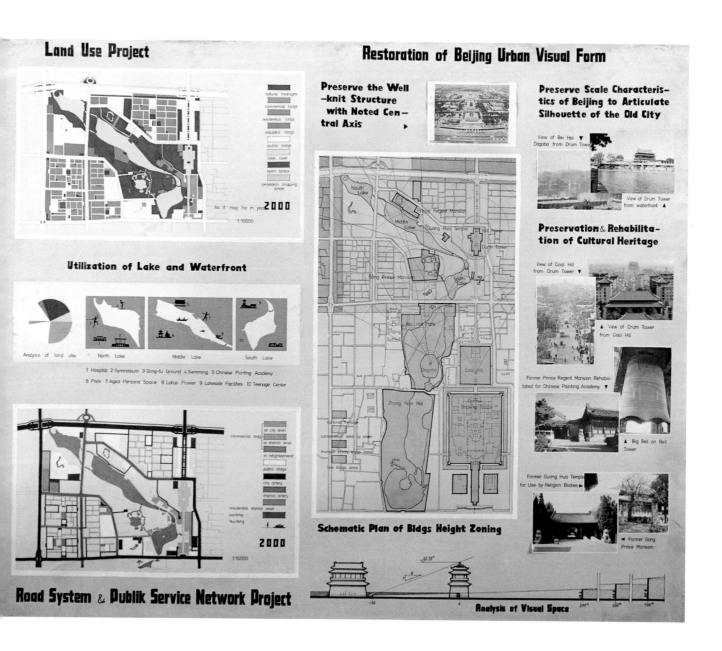

Land Use Project

cultural heritages
commercial bldgs
residential bldgs
industrial bldgs
public bldgs
lake, river
open space
pedestrian shopping street

As it may be in year **2000**

1:10000

Utilization of Lake and Waterfront

Analysis of land use — North Lake — Middle Lake — South Lake

1 Hospital 2 Gymnasium 3 Gong-fu Ground 4 Swimming 5 Chinese Painting Academy
6 Park 7 Aged Persons' Space 8 Lotus Flower 9 Lakeside Facilities 10 Teenage Center

Road System & Publik Service Network Project

commercial bldgs
- at city level
- at district level
- in neighbourhood

public bldgs
city artery
district artery
residential district road
parking
hu-tong

2000

1:10000

Restoration of Beijing Urban Visual Form

Preserve the Well-knit Structure with Noted Central Axis ▶

Preserve Scale Characteristics of Beijing to Articulate Silhouette of the Old City

View of Bei Hai ▼
Dagoba from Drum Tower

View of Drum Tower from waterfront ▲

Preservation & Rehabilitation of Cultural Heritage

View of Coal Hill from Drum Tower ▼

▲ View of Drum Tower from Coal Hill

Former Prince Regent Mansion Rehabilitated for Chinese Painting Academy ▼

▲ Big Bell on Bell Tower

Former Guang Hua Temple for Use by Religion Bodies ▶

◀ Former Gong Prince Mansion

North Lake
Prince Regent Mansion
Middle Lake
Guang Hua Temple
Bell Tower
Drum Tower
Gong Prince Mansion
South Lake
Bei Hai Park
Dagoba
Coal Hill
Zhong Nan Hai
Former Imperial Palace

cultural heritage
conservation area by order
multiple storey bldgs area
low bldgs area

Schematic Plan of Bldgs Height Zoning

Analysis of Visual Space

However, the chosen site had poor prospects of growth from the start. A century later, it was replaced by a new commercial district in the south of the city, which has remained as such to this day. Shichahai district was thus reduced to quarters for the urban poor living in the shadow of great houses.

Since 1949, despite efforts made by the government to provide better housing in the district, rapid industrialisation has brought about population increase and environmental pollution to the further detriment of Shichahai. Courtyard houses meant for single families have been turned into multi-family compounds.

Occasional vacant lots in the neighbourhood are taken up by spontaneous settlers, thus depriving the children of the little remaining play area. Most temples dedicated to the local gods have been converted to cottage industries or small factories. The increasing traffic brings additional chaos to the main shopping street in front of the Drum Tower.

In spite of apparent prosperity achieved since the Liberation, the living standard in the district is still far from satisfactory. The full exploitation of the potentials of the district will not only enhance its mental comfort but also improve the material wellbeing of its inhabitants.

The Guiding Concepts
The proposed redevelopment plan is based on the principles laid down by the masterplan of Beijing:
1 Beijing should be developed to be worthy of the status of a national, political, scientific and cultural centre, as well as a centre for tourism.
2 The containment of the inner city should be strictly adhered to with a planned dispersal of the population of roughly 17 million to 12 million, thereby keeping the population in the urban area to about 5 million.

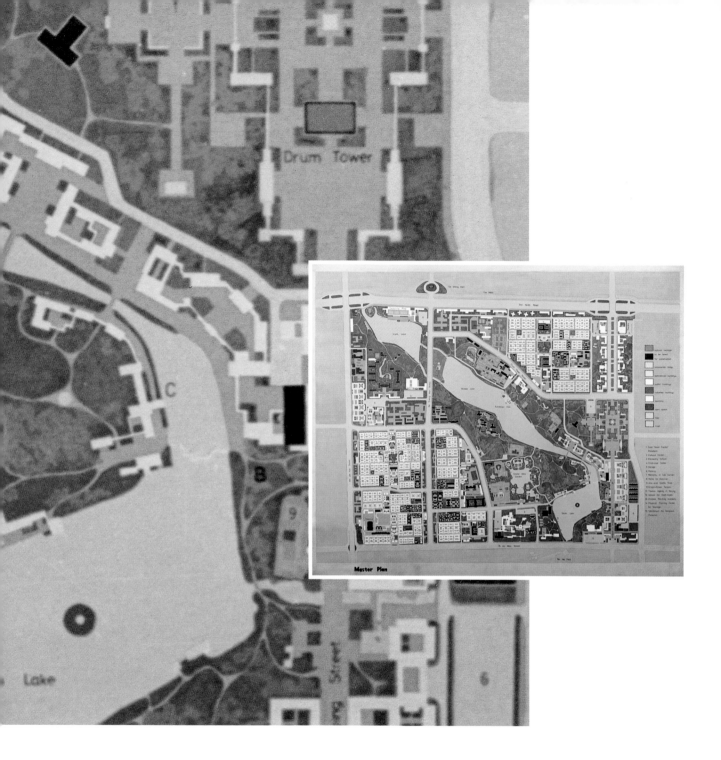

3 There should be strict control of the location and types of existing industries in the urban area. New industries should be excluded from the urban area.

4 Existing industries which are causing pollution and noise with little prospect of immediate improvement are to be relocated elsewhere. The preservation of cultural heritage and conservation of the natural landscape should be enforced rigorously. The Grand Axis of the city should be enhanced to create a unique image of Beijing.

The Structure or Pattern of the Neighbourhood

The establishment of a central axis or 'spine distributor' as in the old system. Childcare facilities, schools, cottage industries, workshops, offices, shops, etc. are to be situated to form a community centre, all within walking distance of the surrounding neighbourhood. The various residential areas will assess the spine distributor through offshoots.

Compounds (neighbourhoods) should incorporate any existing old houses worthy of rehabilitation. Most of the existing properties would have to be cleared or replaced by new housing types developed through assimilation of the virtues, interest and taste of the traditional Chinese courtyard house.

A typical residential compound (neighbourhood) consists of eight two-room units (53 sqm per unit). Each unit will have its own courtyard. Every 10 to 12 dwelling units are planned around a semi public court as a communal space

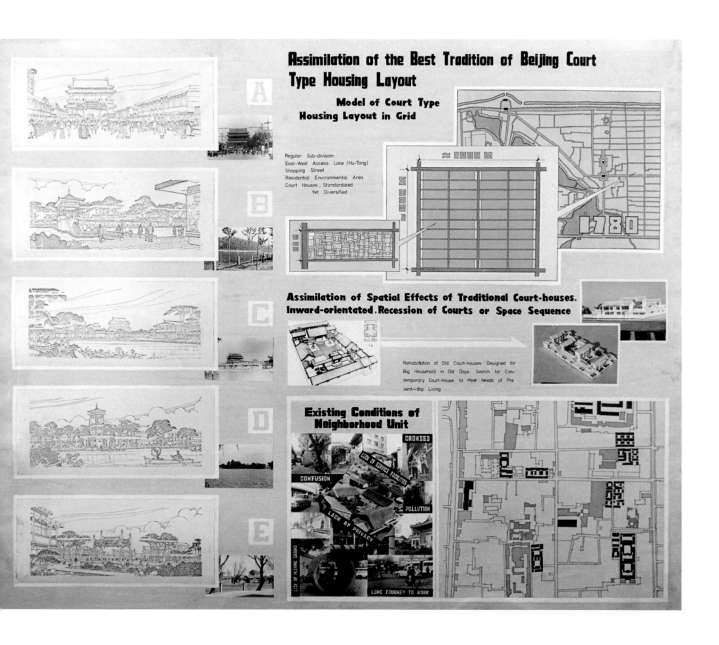

Assimilation of the Best Tradition of Beijing Court Type Housing Layout

Model of Court Type Housing Layout in Grid

Regular Sub-division
East-West Access Lane (Hu-Tong)
Shopping Street
Residential Environmental Area
Court Houses, Standardized
Yet Diversified

Assimilation of Spatial Effects of Traditional Court-houses. Inward-orientated. Recession of Courts or Space Sequence

Rehabilitation of Old Court-houses Designed for Big Household in Old Days. Search for Contemporary Court-house to Meet Needs of Present-day Living

Existing Conditions of Neighborhood Unit

CROWDED
CONFUSION
POLLUTION
LACK OF SERVICE FACILITIES
LACK OF PRIVACY
LACK OF PLAYING GROUND
LONG JOURNEY TO WORK

for the residents. There are to be 115 dwelling units and 540 persons per hectare. In the future the residential density would be 437 persons per hectare.

The development will be of the low-rise-high-density type. Expandability of housing type is aimed at. Each unit should look like a family-house to the users and be harmonious with the environment.

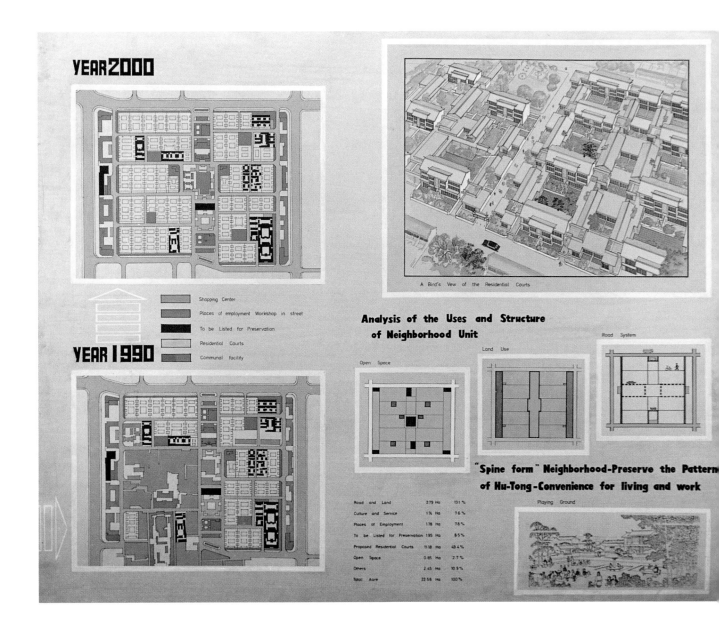

Drum Tower Street Urban Shopping Centre and Lakeside Area

The present Drum Tower Street Shopping Centre is to be developed as a pedestrianised precinct. The traffic will be diverted to a new road to the east.

The existing dwellings around the lake will be demolished for redevelopment. The bank of the Southern Lake adjacent to the pedestrian precinct is to be reserved for entertainment facilities and restaurants. A low-rise hotel with a commanding view of the two Towers is proposed on the opposite bank.

The banks of the Middle Lake are to be landscaped to integrate an existing monastery and three princely mansions into a unified design. Prince Gong's Mansion, commonly acknowledged as the prototype of Daguan Yuan Garden

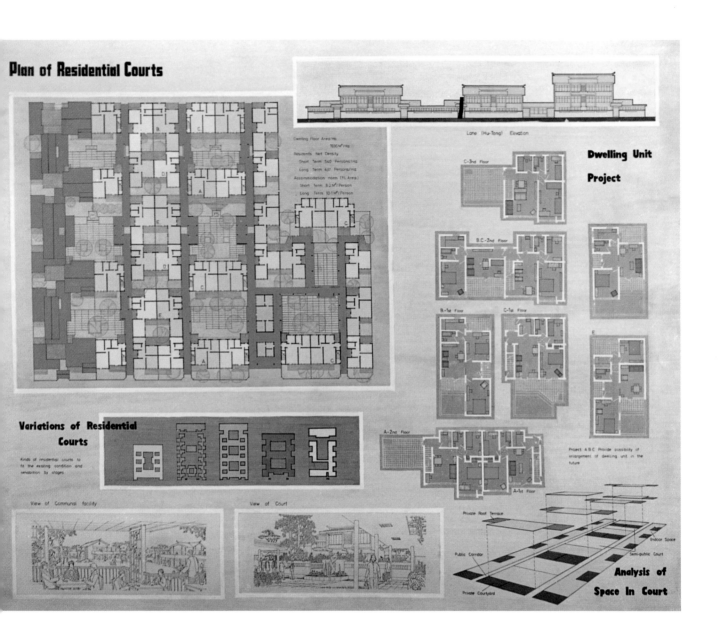

Plan of Residential Courts

Dwelling Unit Project

Variations of Residential Courts

Kinds of residential courts to fit the existing condition and rehabilition by stages.

View of Communal facility

View of Court

Analysis of Space In Court

depicted in the famous Chinese novel *The Dream of the Red Chamber*, is to be rehabilitated as a museum to depict the life described in this great novel.

The orthopaedic hospital built in the early 50's along the Northern Lake is to be remodelled to suit the surrounding traditional roofline. Health and sports facilities are to be developed.

The present is born of the past, and yet the future rests with the present. We are here to reflect on the past, to account for the present, and ultimately to formulate a conscious plan of action for a better and more liveable human habitat of the 21st century.

The world's geographical distances have shrunk, although the regional disparities are growing. Yet this age has endowed all of us with a common mission. It requires us to come to terms with the present, face the challenges, develop a holistic thinking and co-ordinate our efforts.

1   Coming to terms with the Centuries

The 20th century: unparalleled construction and destruction

The 20th century has seen unprecedented magnificence and progress, and also incomparable calamity and confusion. It has enriched the history of architecture in its unique manner: architects have played an admirable role in the reconstruction that followed the two world wars; technical and artistic innovations on a massive scale have introduced fine examples of design to the masses like never before.

But, much of the built environment is still in a deeply unsatisfactory state. The very survival of humanity is under threat amidst the squandering of the world's natural and cultural heritage. In the affluent regions, redevelopment often means destruction by construction; in the poorer areas, pauperised masses are struggling to build their own cities of tomorrow.

Over the past century, the world has turned into a very different place. Yet one thing remains the same: we architects are again at a crossroad of our profession.

The 21st century: a turning point

The diversity and complexity of the world have created much confusion; yet it is but part of the eternal process of change. The present century has seen remarkable reform and development in politics, economics, technology, and society, and the resurgence of human ideas. In the coming century, the pace of transformation is expected to accelerate though its direction may be even harder to tell.

In the coming century, the coexistence of globalisation and pluralism will bring to a head the conflicts and the contradictions that characterise our age. On the one hand, modern means of communications have brought into close contact diverse cultures and traditions; global integration of production, finance and technology continues to dominate decision-making. On the other hand, the gap between the rich and the poor continues to widen at an alarming rate; regional strife and financial uncertainties cast a sinister shadow upon the human habitat.

Whilst we should not take on tasks outside our professional bounds, it would be both irresponsible and foolish to ignore the torrent of social and cultural change that is redefining the scope of the architectural profession. A conscious reconsideration of the role of 21st century architecture calls for our enthusiasm, strength and courage.

2   The challenges that we face

Nature's revenge

The Industrial Revolution unleashed tremendous human power, yet many a triumph over nature was achieved at a harrowing cost. The past century has seen population explosion, encroachment of farmland and deterioration of water, air and land resources. Environmental crises impinge on the very existence of humankind.

We do not know enough about the ecosystem, yet ecological disasters have revealed its fragile confines. From a historical point of view, we do not own the world that we live in: we simply manage it for our children. In what state shall we hand over town and country to our children? In what way can an architect contribute to the future of human civilisation through planning and design?

Overwhelming urbanisation
To better their lives, people congregate in the city, where science, technology and culture have brought about productivity could not have been foreseen. The 20th century saw the brightest lights so far in metropolitan life. Nevertheless, the century ahead is the true urban era, as for the first time in history, urban dwellers will outnumber those who live in traditional rural ways.

Yet, hardly have the slums been demolished, when cities see the resurgence of the underclass. The segregation of the rich and the poor, traffic congestion, land use, and air and noise and pollution have worsened in cities large and small. Can our cities survive? We build the cities; yet we feel powerless when we attempt to make any change. In what way can we shape the urban habitat, as it shapes us at the same time? Will traditional concepts survive in the cities of the next century?

Technology as a double-edged sword
Modern technologyhas increased productivity to a degree never before experienced. New materials, new structures and new equipment have provided unique opportunities for designers of the 20th century. Modern means of communications have brought diverse cultures in close contact.

Technology has led humankind to a new crossroad, yet we are still in the process of harnessing its power and potential. Technology modifies the traditional relationships between man and nature, and thus constantly challenges the existing norms of lifestyles and values. In what way can humankind derive benefits from technology, whilst avoiding the harm it is also capable of?

Genius loci in default
The culture of architecture comes from a local accumulation of history. It manifests itself among the built forms and in day to day living, exerting a voiceless influence on the experience and behaviour of the inhabitants. In a sense, it is the soul of our cities, towns and villages.

However, globalisation of technology has made people more and more separated from their land. Standardised commercial production interrupts the evolution of local built forms. Traditional design techniques are confronted. Local identities fade away. What contribution can an architect make to bring back the soul of cities and towns, which characterised them in the past?

A common theme, a common future
The challenges we face are multifaceted and overwhelming. They are in fact the embodiment of complex social, political, economic and cultural processes at levels local and global. Our discussion must not stop at the mere manifestations of such processes. Rather, an effective solution only comes from a thorough understanding of the dialectic nature of the forces, which are shaping our built environment today.

The search for effective solutions at a global level is supported by our common aspirations for a sustainable future on this planet. Our world is an interdependent world. The future prospect of one nation to a large extent rests on the future of other nations. By the same token, the future of architecture depends on an understanding and assimilation of the achievements of other disciplines and professions. It is this common theme that will bring us together to lay out a common future for the 21st century.

3   Towards an integral architecture

During the past 50 years, architects of the world have debated over a large number of issues. These debates have furthered our understanding in all branches of architecture. It is therefore appropriate to review the progress so far and redefine the limits, the contents, and the organisation of our discipline and profession.

The theoretical premises
The role of an architect is constantly modified to suit the needs and requirements of the times. Where traditional methods are inadequate, new approaches have been developed to take their place. Yet without exception, each redefinition pushes the boundary of architecture outwards to wider coverage, as well as inwards to higher degrees of specialisation. The 20th century is perhaps the most exemplary in this regard.

The 20th century architect is empowered with unprecedented professional opportunities and potential, yet at a personal level, an expanding profession with growing specialisation can seem elephantine. In a sense, the architects' Tower of Babel appears to have fallen: it is increasingly difficult for one architect to grasp the expertise of a fellow architect; although the body of knowledge has grown collectively, the outlook of any single designer tends to become paradoxically narrow and fragmented. Specialised expertise is brought together through financial ties and managerial skills, rather than a coherent intellectual framework. As a result, the role of an architect continues to be marginalised in decision-making over the human habitat today.

From the point of view of an architect, his or her ability to propose creative design solutions depends critically on the intellectual and professional spheres he or she commands. Narrow and fragmented individual outlooks cannot work, however wonderfully the individual designers are managed externally. Nevertheless, any given person cannot and should not attempt to master the whole body of knowledge of our profession. Quo vadis?

The classical Chinese philosophers took pains to pinpoint the differences between "methodology" (alternatively translated as *dao* or *tao*) which concerns the intellectual framework, and "methods" (*fa*) which deals with specific techniques. It is useful to draw on their wisdom on this matter. Whatever professional talents, expertise, or preferences an architect may have, they can only realise their true value when guided by a larger, intellectual perspective. An architect may work in a specialised area by choice or chance, yet he or she must not lose sight of the larger whole of the profession, and the vast sphere of knowledge, which is potentially at his or her disposal.

Past and contemporary masters have shown how their understanding of the *dao* of architecture has helped them to achieve magnificent heights in design and planning. If such understanding is regarded as a luxury enjoyed by the masters in the past, it will increasingly become necessary for all architects in this age of information explosion. In the rapidly expanding professional universe, an intellectual orientation that organises knowledge and expertise and relates architecture to the wider processes that give shape to the built environment is paramount.

So what does this methodology contain?

A fusion of architecture, landscape architecture and city planning
The professional identity of an architect in the wider world focuses on the built forms that are ultimately created.

Basically, the general theory of architecture is an integration of architecture, landscape and urban planning with city design at its core. However, the increasing scale and scope of modern development provide architects with great opportunities to deal with architecture, landscape and urban planning as a whole. This tripartite composition enables the designer to search for solutions within a wider sphere.

Architecture as a process for the human habitat
Since architecture deals with human settlement, it should regard the physical objectives of construction as a system of circulation. The life-cycle of buildings should be regarded as a fundamental factor of design. It not only includes the construction and running phases, but also processes aimed at lower resource costs, less pollution and grey energy consumption, recycling as much as possible, and reformation of environments.

On the aspect of urban settlement, factors such as planning, architectural design, historical preservation, adaptive re-use of old buildings, urban rehabilitation, city renewal and reconstruction, utilisation of underground facilities should be integrated into a dynamic circulation system. This is a system for better architecture under the modern space-times of architecture. It is also an exemplification of the sustainable approach in urban planning and architectural design.

Multiple technology rooted in the indigenous cultures
Utilising technological innovation to its fullest is one of our basic tasks in the coming century.

In the 21st century, various presentations of technology will co-exist, based on the fact that there are regional contrasts and imbalances in the development of technology.

Theoretically, it is necessary to adopt new technology from foreign sources, and integrate it with local condition, to improve the local technological standards. If architects themselves know the ecological challenges mankind is facing, and adopt advanced technology creatively then the buildings they design ought to be sustainable and healthy.

For each project, the choice of technology should be made according to its own conditions. Different forms of technology should be integrated, utilised and improved.

Considerations of human, ecological, economic and regional aspects should be integrated. Different levels of innovation should be carried out in order to improve the level of architectural creativity.

The development of technology must be related to human factors. As Alvar Aalto said, "the preservation of difference should also be strengthened". The development of architecture should be rooted in the regional background, and local conditions taken as its starting point in the search for better solutions. Based on this, foreign ideas can be integrated into our own. This would finally lead to a human society of both integrity and variety.

Architecture of harmony instead of monotony
Architecture is by definition a regional product: buildings serve, and derive their significance from local contacts. Regional architecture is by no means a mere product of a region's past. Rather, it is derived from the concerns for its future. The significance of our profession lies in the creative designs that bridge the past and the future. We use our professional knowledge to guide an informed choice amongst the options that are increasingly open to local communities. "The sharing of experiences among various countries and geographical regions must never be seen as a simple transfer of ready made solutions, but as a means of stimulating local imaginations."

The localisation of modern architecture and the modernisation of local architecture is a common approach to be shared by all in the progress towards architecture proliferation.

Art for the sake of the built environment
The Industrial Revolution has resulted in dramatic changes in urban structure and architectural forms. The physical environment is anarchic. We should try to find order out of this anarchy, to find beauty and harmony out of chaos.

To consider the relationship between architecture and its environments with the traditional design methods is far from adequate. We have to look at architecture from a macro urban view. Architectural thoughts should shift from single buildings to building complexes, to urban and rural regional planning. The holistic relationship with nature is another important factor that should be considered.

Architecture as the ultimate manifestation in the fine arts, such as sculpture, painting, craftsmanship, should be one of our goals.

Architecture for all
In many traditional societies, the architect played the part of master co-ordinator of all building trades. Yet today, by a large majority, the architect is perceived as a style freak, irrelevant to real decision-making. It is appropriate to view architecture in its full socio-political context, rather than in the narrow techno-aesthetic sense of the term. Only in this way, can architects "participate at all levels of decision-making as professionals".

Architects should expand their professional services and visions. They should take an active part in social reform with a basic understanding of the society and a respect for the people. It is an architect's destiny to provide shelter for the poor and the homeless. The freedom of architectural design is by no means an excuse of ignorance of social responsibilities.

Architecture is a science that serves the people. A society-wide understanding and participation of architecture will be very helpful to make better environments. Not only should the end users participate in the design process, but also the decision-makers. Support and policies from governments will be especially effective.

The cultural and architectural education of the decision-maker is a determining factor for the quality of a building project. In this sense, the understanding of architecture should be emphasised in every society.

Learning architecture

The future of architecture lies in an architectural education that results in the growth of the new generation of architects. Architects and architecture students must have a responsible professional spirit and a comprehension of environmental ethics. They should work for the benefit of the society as a whole, and implement strategies that contribute to the overall quality of human settlements.

Architectural education must expand its concerns. An open system of knowledge should be set up. The goal of architectural education is to have a student able to learn, research, express and organise. The student should be encouraged to be open-minded, to utilise new technological advances, and to create on a base of professional knowledge.

Architectural education is life-long. The education of environmental awareness should start in kindergartens, continue in middle schools, professional schools and adult educational instituitions.

Towards an integral architecture

It is necessary to re-emphasis half a century later now the words from Walter Gropius, whose idea of the architect is a co-ordinator "whose business is to unify various formal, technical, social and economic problems that arise in connection with buildings. ... I believe that new architecture is to dominate a far more comprehensive sphere than building means today. And from the investigation of the details, we shall advance towards an ever-wider and profounder conception of design as one great cognate whole."

The development of architecture asks for both analysis and integration. But now, we should focus on integration. The introduction of General Theory of architecture does not demand architects to be professionals with all abilities (which is impossible), but require them to have better professional knowledge and better ways of thinking, in order to be better problem solvers and theory developers.

We are facing a world that is full of contradictions. The contrasts between globalisation and localisation, internationalism and nationalism, universality and particularity, flexibility and stability, etc., are forever increasing. The future development of architecture needs our understanding and processing of these contradictions. Any contemporary building project can be regarded as a collection of the contradictions above. An architect is to deal with these contradictions professionally, to decide between freedom and rules, art and science, the traditional and modern, heritage and innovation, technology and place, assimilation and diversity, etc. The General Theory of architecture is a dialectal process of these contradictions.

4   All pathways for a common destiny

The objective world is interwoven with change and variety. It is neither possible nor desirable to search for identical technical solutions. For centuries, holistic thinking has been the cornerstone of the Eastern philosophies. Today it is becoming a common heritage and blessing of the global village: "For all the means in the world there is but one end, for all the concerns there is but one destiny."

Our concerns may lead us to the following conclusions:
Firstly, searching the point of integration in a world of interwoven complexities.
Many ancient Chinese philosophical and literary sayings emphasised the importance of integration and holistic thinking.

20th century architecture has celebrated its triumphs and miracles, but these are mere fragments of history. To lead the architecture of a new era to a common destiny, we should try to find out those fragments in history that did make unique contributions, that made milestones in human civilisation. With the integration of those fragments, and a return to our basic concerns, we may find the spirit of the new architecture, the doctrine of the new era, and the opportunity of new creations for the 21st century.

Secondly, different ways lead to a common destination.
Given the regional contrasts, every nation should have its own particular way of development. Only with these 'different ways', can the human civilisation continue in a sustainable manner.

As the old Western saying goes, "Every road leads to Rome". There may be no common roads, but there is a common future. The future of mankind living in a blessed environment.

The architect should, therefore, devote his or her life in the pursuance of humanism, quality, capability and creativity. It is his or her responsibility to build up a better environment with the limited natural resources on this planet.

At the turn of the century, we have grasped the theme of the new era, have found out the basic contradictions, and are reaching for the concurrence of our agenda. It should be seen that the beginning of the new century is only a spot in the continuous thread of civilisation.

The research we are doing today is only the beginning co-ordination of mankind for our common goal, a beginning that is supposed to make changes. We look forward with caution and optimism, to the historic duty of building the 21st century human habitat. We are prepared for a new exploration of common themes and methodologies. From this standpoint, we look forward to the future and to the mission that will reshape the future.

Paper delivered at the Jubilee of the Union of International Architects, 20th Congress, Beijing, China, June 1999.

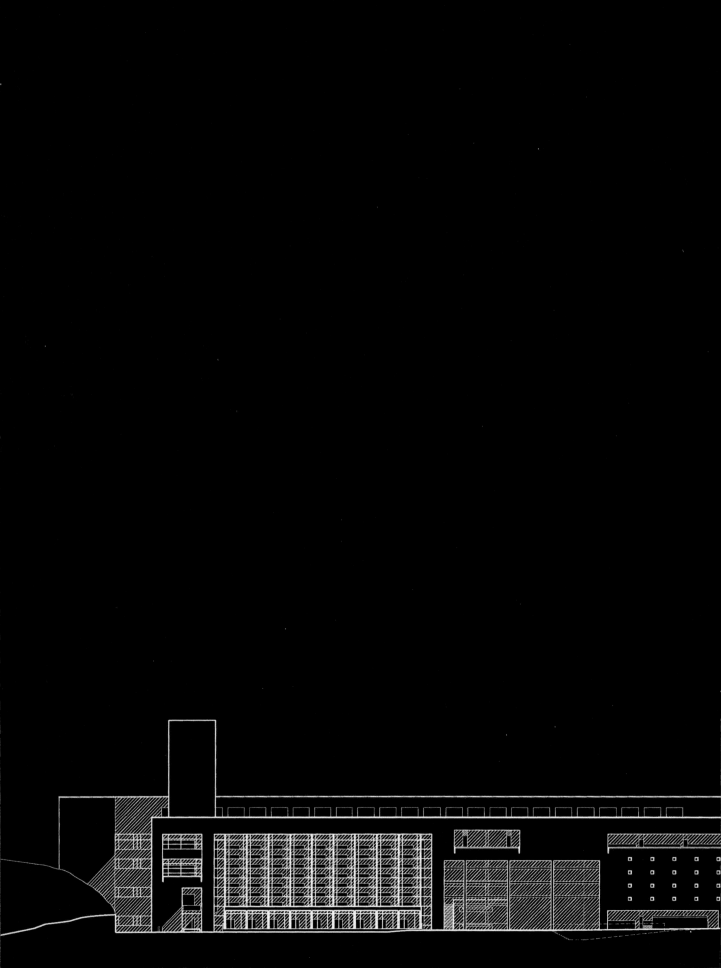

Min Hyunsik ___

Abstracting the Geography of the Land

Figurine on a base,
A. Giacometti, 1994

Bust of Diego,
A. Giacometti, 1995

Chong Seock Jeong,
a black and white
drawing, Jeoung Sun

Berlin Philharmonic Hall, H. Scharoun

One of the most generalised views about architecture is that its *raison d'être* is in its space rather than its form. Le Corbusier has defined architecture as "the masterly, correct and magnificent play of masses (spaces), brought together in light[1] while Louis Kahn put importance on the space of continual astonishment that changes along with the quality of light. The space I am referring to, as referred to in the words of Le Corbusier or Kahn, is that between concrete forms – the emptiness itself. It is this invisible emptiness that provides a ground for various events which, along with space, is the main concern of my work. The "otherness" of things is the influence they radiate onto their surroundings[2]. The very fact that it is capable of existing – the fact that it does exist, that it is not crushed, scrubbed, seems to indicate that there is a force which maintains it. This force is not simply an internal energy, but is an outgoing one that has an impact on its surroundings.

This attitude tends to adopt a dichotomous view of phenomena and essence. Or, in contrast, one thoroughly concentrated on phenomena or the unconscious which controls it. We are provided, however, with an artistic intuition to overcome these limitations in the words of Alberto Giacometti, who succeeded in a dialectic unification of these issues:

> "I have often felt in front of living beings – above all, in front of human heads – the sense of space atmosphere which immediately surrounds these beings, penetrates them, is already the being themselves."

Thus the value of Giacometti's works are found not in the other-worldly quality of their figures, but in the wholeness that encompasses the figures and the empty space between them. This quality is shared by Oriental paintings as well – the white areas, those spared from the act of painting, are acknowledged as the most crucial and difficult parts.

Let us now depart from recent architectural trends that are so much confined to their visual objects, i.e. forms, and start anew by designing the space between forms rather than the forms, and giving importance to the events which take place in those spaces.

1 Le Corbusier, *Towards a New Architecture*, Preager Pub
2 C H Waddington, *Behind Appearance*, Edinburgh University
3 Michael Benedict, *For an Architecture of Reality*, Lumen Books

alk Institute, L. Kahn   L. Baragan house, L. Baragan   Byoungsan-Seowon   Piazza del Compo, Sienna

The way Hans Scharoun broke the conventional composition of a music hall comes to mind. In explaining his Berlin Philharmonic Hall, where the division between a stage and seats no longer exists, he made it clear that the point of departure for its design already transcended traditional approach: "The idea of this architecture has stemmed from the event of a concert rather than formal aesthetics. The occurrence of playing the music and experiencing them was to take place in a single whole space."

In those rare instances when these events become metaphysical or spiritual, we experience the value of emptiness speaking for itself: the plaza that opens toward the Pacific in Kahn's Salk Institute; the gardens that open to the sky in the houses by Luis Barragan; and the view of Nakdong River and Mt Byoungsan behind the columns of the Byoungsan-Seowon, all exemplify the significance of emptiness.

Michael Benedict has described the aesthetic of emptiness as follows: "The word emptiness has a set of connotations not intended here – that sick and hollow feeling of loss or loneliness, the pain of hunger, and so forth. What is meant by emptiness here is rather more like... silence, clarity, and transparency. Emptiness may resound without sound, may be filled by its potential to be filled, and make open what is complete... Emptiness is more akin to the idea of space, or interval. It is in the gaps between stepping stones, in the silence between notes in music... when a child's swing reaches a point of neither rising nor falling and is momentarily weightless.[3]

Important elements of architecture which accentuate this emptiness are the structure, fabric and system of the mat. Compared with the electronic microchip, these do not have a fixed beginning or end, but is essentially in a constant flow of mobility. Contemporary sports, based on fluid-like flowing media, also share common features: hang-gliding, bungee-jumping, surfing, and rafting tend to be highly varied, changing, unpredictable, requiring sharp sensibility, quick judgment and calculated risks.

Likewise, the mat is not a product designed in accordance with function; it is a temporary material corresponding to changing situations of the space or place, determined by the method of the user's occupancy. The Piazza del Campo of Sienna provides an early example: its full realisation of possibility can be found in the sloped plaza of the Pompidou Centre in Paris, and similar ideas are notable behind the competition entry project of the Nara Culture Center by Florian Beigel and Kim Jong-kyu, the Jussieu Library by Rem Koolhaas, and the Mat Building of Allison and Peter Smithson.

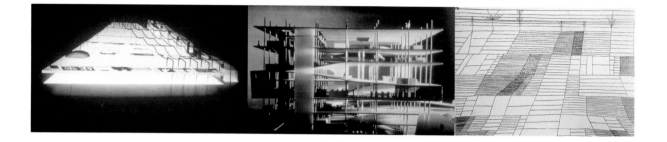

Nara Cultural Center, competition entry,
F. Biegel & Kim Jong-kyu

Jussieu Library, R. Koolhaas

Landscape, P. Klee

The reference of the mat is the land; its archetype is the landscape which the land creates. What we are concerned is not the natural, untouched space in its primary form, but rather the artificially transfigured or culturalised surface. For its process of fragmentation and integration reveals the quintessence of natural phenomena. We find its examples in the abstraction of Paul Klee's landscapes, Richard Long's earth art, the Korean traditional calligraphy by Chusa Kim Jung-hee, and the later paintings by Suhwa Kim Hwan-kee. Nature gone through the process of artificialisation and culturalisation is the abstracted output of primitive nature, extracting its essential orders.

Cultivated through a long period of time, thus becoming intimate to nature and itself emerging as another kind, the space created by the land offers a fine textbook to architecture design. W G Hoskins, an English historian, once mentioned that it is lucky to be born in England, where nothing much has changed for the last few centuries. Presumably it is because, through the abstracted landscape of the land, they can trace the vestiges of life which convey the wisdom of their forefathers. This is exactly why we are attentive to the space of our land.

The spatial fabric of our landscape is most clearly seen in our ancient maps. What especially characterises the cartography of the late Chosun period is its emphasis on the chain of mountains; mountains are never depicted as separated entities but as continuously linked flow. Though drawn on a plane, the mountains and valleys display three-dimensional space, showing the flows of rivers and mountains. They exhibit the aspects of life such as cultivating, building houses and forming villages, adjusted to the characters of our land. Furthermore, to the perceptive eye, they go on to present our ancestors' view about nature and the world. We have conceived the sky, the land and man as an organic whole: an integration of early Confucianism, Taoist Naturalism, and Zen Buddhism has generated a philosophy of coexistence between man and nature. The land was considered as a living being, representing nature where man is another component. It actively participates in the growth of things: the vitality with which the land performs in this process was believed to determine the good or ill fortune of man. Whereas the contemporary geography comprehends the land as a mere lifeless matter submitted to the use of man, our traditional thoughts accepted it as a dynamic existence, whose strength directly influenced man's life. The so-called Myungdang, or fine places, is where these energy is concentrated, a location of ultimate harmony in nature.

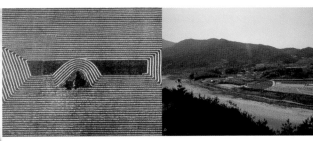

Mirage, a line in the Sahara,
, Long

A landscape

DaeDongYeoJiDo, part of
Seoul, Kim Jeongho

A landscape

Town of HanGye,
Sanchung, Kyungnam

Our predecessors have reified this view on nature in the artificialisation and abstraction of the land into the spatial fabric of landscape: surrounding the rear with the mountains and facing the flow of water, the fields are gradually stepped down along with the topography of land. These typical performances of abstraction are now our references for good design.

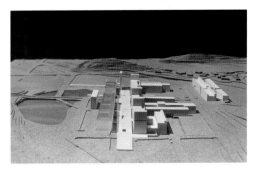

National Museum of Korea, honorable mention
of the competition, Min Hyunsik & Seung Hyosang,
1996.

Sindo-Ricoh Factory

Ahsan, South Korea, 1994.

The site was not in an ideal condition for a factory: since it was a low hill heavily cut and filled, locations of each building were separated by heights over 10m, generating large and precipitous retaining walls, and were connected by steep roads.

The largest portion of the land was obviously the site for the main factory, and other accompanying facilities had to be dispersed over the remaining areas. This limited condition led to their narrow and long shapes, with immense height differences. This, however, was compensated by the grand vistas it provided, and even implied various architectural possibilities, such as direct accessibility from the ground to two or more storeys.

The site of the headquarters was also narrow and long, with a height difference of 7.5m from the existing factory, and 6m from the entrance road, but commanded a fine view on the northwest facing the Hyunchungsa, looking down on the great plains of Tangjung. These circumstances has inspired a few architectural ideas: the first was the intentional narrowing of the Madang that mediates the headquarters and the factory. A carefully arranged dimension of 16m-wide, 96m-long, and 16m-height

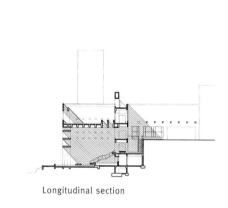

Longitudinal section

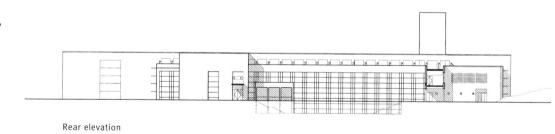

Rear elevation

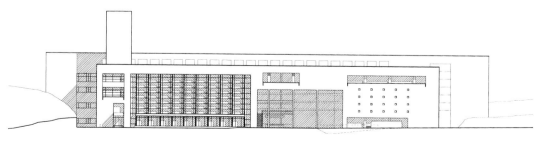

Front elevation

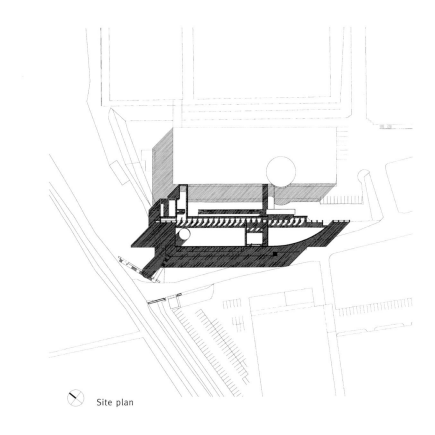

Site plan

intensifies tension of the space which is released upwards to the Santae-sanjung on the south. It will provide the users of the facility a chance to break away from everyday life and make time for meditation. The next object concerned the design of a three-dimensional link between the Madang's upper and lower levels. By carving out the middle of the building that lies across the narrow site, and filling it with vertical and horizontal paths, we could lessen the labour of walking up and down to different levels, and amuse them through the dramatic spatial characteristics. The effect is all the more heightened as the sunlight hits upon the adjacent pond and waterfall. Third intention was exploring, as done with the exterior, the full dimensions of indoor spaces. The cafeteria and the auditorium, the two main spaces of the lower floor, reach up to the height of two storeys. Through these interlocking, penetrating spaces pass the circulating lines that integrate the whole space. The magnificent play of spaces is amplified by simple colours and materiality of the surfaces that also lend itself as a grand canvas to the twilight.

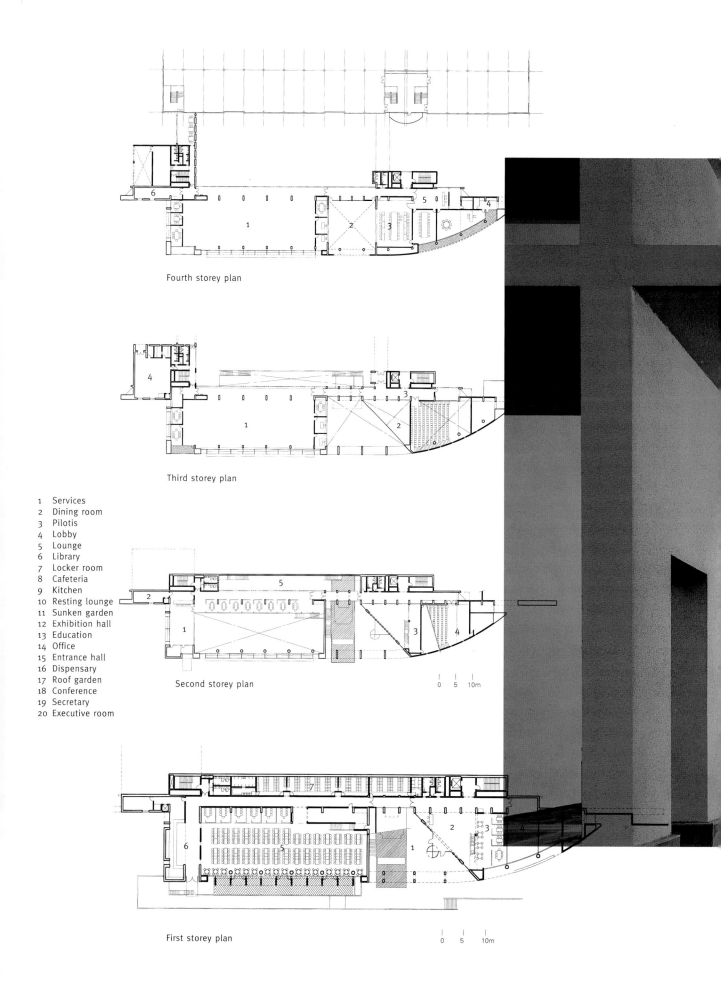

Fourth storey plan

Third storey plan

1 Services
2 Dining room
3 Pilotis
4 Lobby
5 Lounge
6 Library
7 Locker room
8 Cafeteria
9 Kitchen
10 Resting lounge
11 Sunken garden
12 Exhibition hall
13 Education
14 Office
15 Entrance hall
16 Dispensary
17 Roof garden
18 Conference
19 Secretary
20 Executive room

Second storey plan

0   5   10m

First storey plan

0   5   10m

Hostel for Sindo-Ricoh Workers

Ahsan, South Korea, 1991.

My recent architectural interest centres on "neutral space" and "emptiness". The former is about the function of a space and the latter is about the aesthetics of space.

These ideas basically come from a conviction that the character of architecture depends on the manner in which it is lived in, that is to say how a space is occupied by people. A space under certain specific conditions produces a unique feeling and emotion. Thus it is critical for the architect to be conscious of what he expects to see in his building under changing conditions. A good example of this consciousness could be found in the empty courtyard of any Korean traditional house (*madang*).

This hostel for the Sindo-Ricoh workers stands alone in the middle of a vast rice field. This rice field changes its environment during four seasons, in spring it is a lake, in summer it is a meadow, in fall it is a golden carpet and in winter, a white blanket.

The workers pass through the field at different moments of day and night: some workers work from 8 a.m. to 4 p.m. to midnight while some work from midnight to 8 a.m. Each worker would have different impressions of the rice field in each specific moment of time.

I have therefore made a significant "wall" which always welcome them when they return from the battlefield of work with tired bodies and souls.

The wall absorbs and reflects the changes in every specific environmental condition, and it energetically tries to hold together the family of rooms.

1 Main entrance
2 Lounge
3 Resting lounge
4 Dining room
5 Kitchen
6 Service entrance
7 Storage
8 Package-unit room
9 Room
10 Corridor

First storey plan

0   5   10m

Sungyak Presbyterian Church

Euijoungboo, South Korea 1997.

The site lies next to the Kyungwon railroad. Like most regions adjacent to railroad stations in a small city, this place has left and still displays the traces of the past, going as far back as the Korean War. It is a back-street, poverty-stricken, neglected from the contemporary developments, erected along the city's main road just a block away.

The beauty of these buildings, however, is merely skin-deep: apart from their facades, they also reveal dim images which make possible only the addition of cheap motels and bars. An atmosphere of immorality and malevolence is drenched along this whole area.

Hence our primary question: what meaning does a church convey in this context? What could be the obligation of the Christian community in such conditions?

What we had was a desolate railroad with the accompanying noise, and beyond it a beautiful scenery of Mt Dobong. Its legendary peaks and chains towards the north proudly exhibit their full grandeur in the morning, and at dusk form a silhouette of curvilinear ridge-line behind the crimson sky.

Open to the railroad and the peaks of Mt Dobong, we have laid a narrow garden, or *madang*, with a deep space. It connects two levels with a traditional method of steps, not by blocking but exposing itself to the sounds of the railroad, it reminds the visitors that we are in fact just visitors in life also. This, along with the grand view of Mt Dobong, would hopefully make this a blessed place of pilgrimage, enabling our minds to perceive the world of origin.

The main program of this church is of course the place for services. It is well known that the Christian religion, with the approval of Constantinus in the 4th century, had risen above ground from the catacombs and set its chapel in a basilica. This marked the beginning of church architecture which, after 2000 years, has not been changed significantly. The Reformation of the 16th century or the magnificent revolution of Modernism has all failed to provide an alternative to the basilica plan of the churches.

With this project, we discreetly set to question this long tradition: a reconsideration of the essential forms of the Protestant Church. Why does the altar, which has long lost its meaning, occupy the most important space? Why does the hierarchical division of sanctum and nave still prevail, and why do the attending devotees relate only to its sanctums? Why not form a relationship between the devotees? In other words, our new proposal on the spatial composition of the church was that of a place where every attendant could build a relationship with one another and form a unification, and where each could stand equal to and directly meet God. This seemed highly appropriate to the doctrines of Protestantism, especially Calvinism. It was a sort of architectural objection to the disappointing tendency of the Korean Protestant in the deification or, in some cases, idolisation of the church's authority and its consequential regression to the practices of the Roman Catholic Church.

Placing the activities of sermon and giving praise in the centre and dividing the nave on each side facing each other, the whole can become one integrated space without hierarchy. Acts of giving and receiving the sermon, praising and listening, saying and attending prayers, confessions and dedications thus could be made in a single space. The distribution of light was also equally arranged, and ornaments were thoroughly excluded.

On the layout of the site, the *madang* and the chapel occupy carefully balanced positions, whose between is filled with views of the railroad and the mountain peaks; it was an insertion of an extraordinary scene in the juxtaposition of two events or activities. I regard the only thing to be preserved eternally in a church to be the service of Christians in a single space and having heartfelt conversations with God. Hopefully this work proves to be faithful to my belief.

Parts of this text were inspired by the conversation with J Sillett, F Beigel, and J K Kim.

East elevation

West elevation

0 5 10m

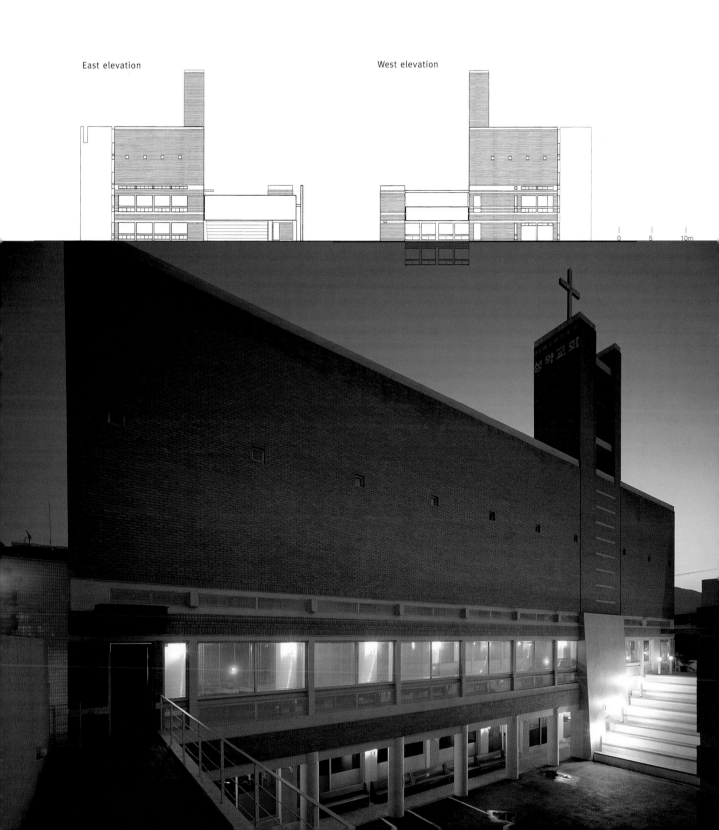

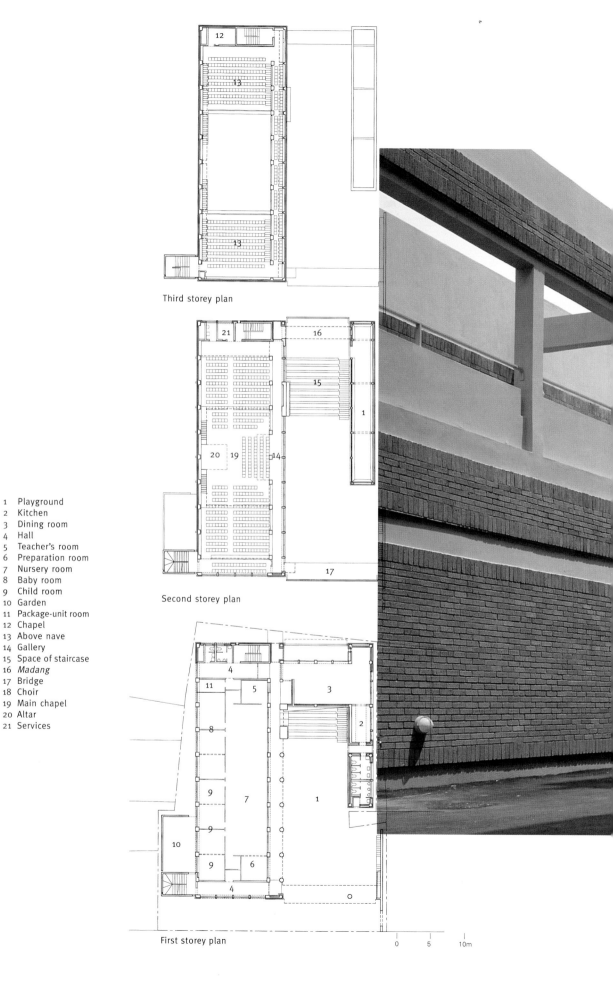

Third storey plan

Second storey plan

1 Playground
2 Kitchen
3 Dining room
4 Hall
5 Teacher's room
6 Preparation room
7 Nursery room
8 Baby room
9 Child room
10 Garden
11 Package-unit room
12 Chapel
13 Above nave
14 Gallery
15 Space of staircase
16 *Madang*
17 Bridge
18 Choir
19 Main chapel
20 Altar
21 Services

First storey plan

0   5   10m

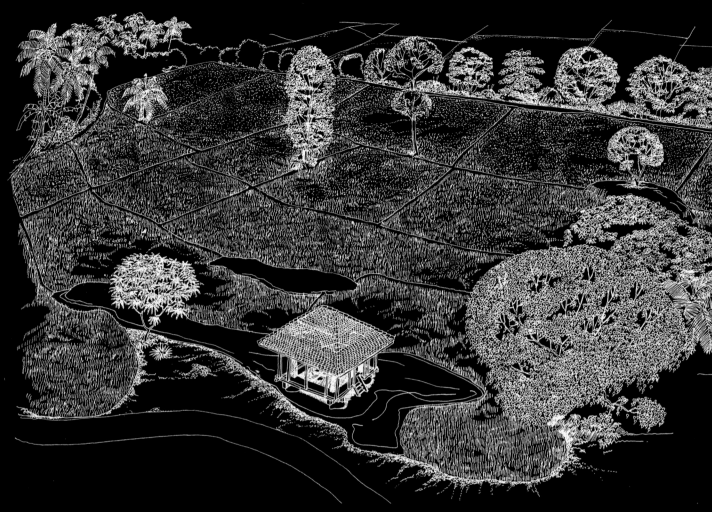

24-10-88 - Channa
Ambalama at Karagahagedera
Kurunegala district.

"You knew me well if you thought that by its very excess virtue entice me.
You knew that arduous and challenging paths lure me,
that senseless pursuits appeal to me...,
and that a little folly is necessary for the satisfaction of my pride."

André Gide

C. Anjalendran

An Architecture of Dignity

I have a studio with two to three assistants. Until six years ago I practised architecture off my mother's verandah. My office is still "folded away" each day, but now off my own verandah.

I returned to Sri Lanka twenty years ago, having completed post-graduate studies in London. Back home, I was fascinated by the central question facing Sri Lankan architecture — the continuity and the context of the traditional in relation to modern lifestyles and aspirations. The sound political policy in the early 60s of restrictions on import of goods and travel abroad brought about a creative blossoming in the local architecture of Geoffrey Bawa and Ulrik Plesner, in the colourful handlooms of Barbara Sansoni, the vibrant batiks of Ena de Silva and the inimitable architectural renderings of Laki Senanayake.

Unlike all other arts which may portray the contradictions of daily life in particular with under-development and terrorism, architecture must celebrate life. I am weary of an architecture which is merely serious or even just a facade, devoid of the wit and humour of life. I also dislike insensitive impositions on the landscape.

Given such considerations, I guess it should not come as a surprise that I have chosen not to do a commercial sort of architecture, concentrating rather in evolving an economical aesthetic of everyday life. Here I find an affinity to the unpretentious and often unnoticed peasant vernacular. An excellent example is the little crest-shaped pavilion or *ambalama* at Karagahagedera in Kurunagale. This *ambalama* supported on four boulders perched on a large shallow rock at the edge of rice-fields epitomises my architectural ideal.

K. Coomaraswamy, who at the turn of this century explained Asian art to the west as well as the east, stated that the ultimate purpose of all art is to transcend to the level of godhead. For me, it is enough if it provides a meditative refuge from the trauma, the tragedy and the occasional bomb in Sri Lanka.

View of entrance

Anjalendran House
Battaramulla, Sri Lanka, 1993.

I have always wanted a barn for a studio, a gallery and a central courtyard which is the main focus of the house. The colours for the house were provided by Barbara Sansoni, which adds to the meditative ambience. The vast tent-like roof provides good acoustic for Indian ragas and Gregorian chants.

View of living area

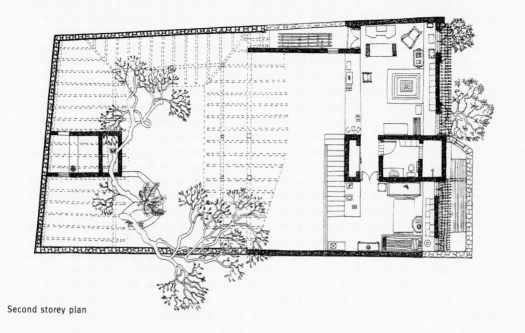

Second storey plan

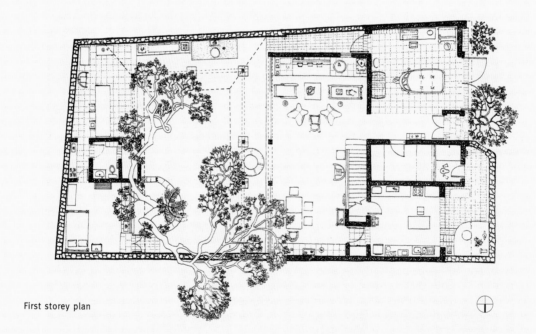

First storey plan

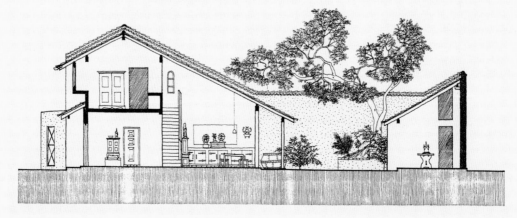

Section

0	5	10m

Above: View of central courtyard   Below: View of central courtyard from dining area

1   Entrance building
2   Flood stream reservation
3   SOS boys' youth facility
4   Community house
5   Hermann Gmeiner
    social centre

Site Plan

0   10   20m

SOS Children's Village
Anuradapura, Sri Lanka, 1996.

SOS is an organisation providing care for orphans and destitute children. The central figure is the 'mother' who brings up ten children in her own house. Hence these children would have cousins, aunts, and grandparents. Such a home is called a 'family house' and is the basic unit of an SOS village. Anuradapura is in the dry north central zone of Sri Lanka. The SOS Children's Village here has a nucleus of fourteen 'family houses' which are arranged around a central green. Each 'family house' has a low modest entrance that opens up to reveal a vast tent-like pre-cast RC roof within. The entrance building is at one end of this 'necklace' that visually connects to the long front verandah of the community house. The community house has a central dining hall with a guest wing and aunts' (who assist 'mothers' when they are unwell) wing, each separated by a courtyard. Jam-fruit trees within these courts allow for shade, breeze and attract birds. To facilitate the 'mothers' and children of an SOS village to integrate into the local community, SOS provides neighbourhood facilities that are necessary in these communities. The segregated triangular corner houses the kindergarten and the community club. The central courtyard of the kindergarten allows for secure supervision. The 'fun animal' seats and see-saws are carved by a crafts co-operative under the guidance of Ena de Silva.

Below: View of entrance building   Above: Detail of central courtyard of entrance building

Front elevation

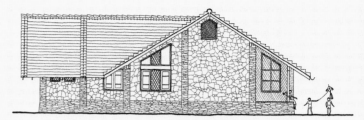

Side elevation

Transverse section

Longitudinal section

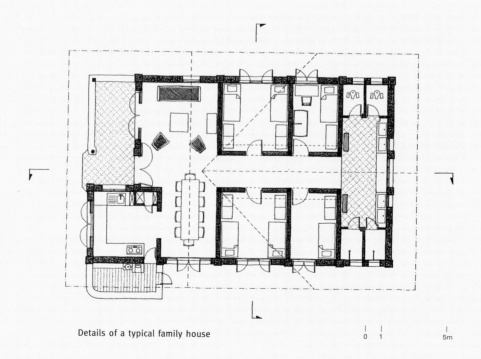

Details of a typical family house

0   1   5m

Opposite: Interior view of a family house

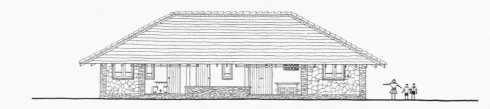

Side elevation

Front elevation

Longitudinal section

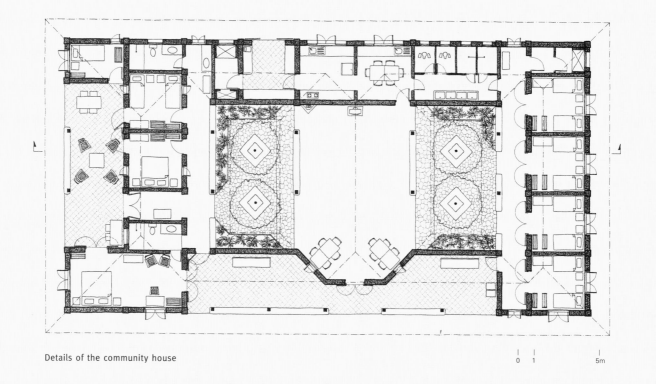

Details of the community house

```
 |  |              |
 0  1              5m
```

Opposite (top): View of the SOS Village from the entrance building   (Below): Front verandah of community house

View of central court from uppermost terrace

Jewellery Making Lapidary and Offices
Nugegoda, Sri Lanka, 1994.

The Client requested a subtle entrance, a secure building, and a pleasant and comfortable working environment for their staff. The last request made this project appealing to me. The main focus of this inverted 'prison' is the central courtyard. This is overlooked by terraces at each level which are edged with cantilevered planters. These terraces are stepped back in an outward spiral. This makes the perception of the central space distinctly different at each level.

Section   0 1   5m

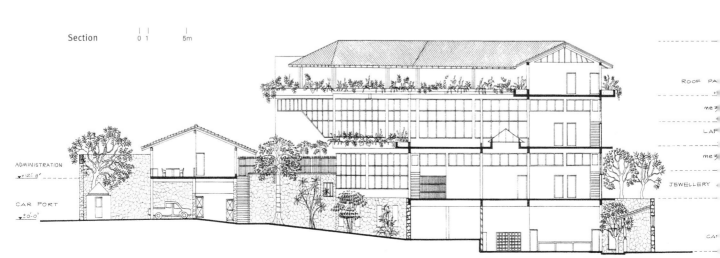

View of central court with stepped-back terraces

Dining area at ground level

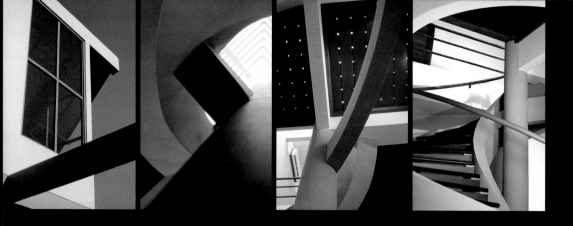

A building has a life which is separate from whatever perspectives we may have of it. It exists simultaneously within and beyond the criteria of its intended users. It has to be conceived to possess multiple potential identities. There exists a plurality in the assimilation of any building from one individual to another. I endeavour to express this actively in my work by redefining the programme, the idiom, perceptions and to move beyond sheer vocabulary in order to achieve an architecture which can have multiple interpretations and renditions in different frames of reference, both present and future.

I think it is naive to assume a universal model for architecture (or anything for that matter), or simple reductive laws governing it. The nature of the world is not like that in my experience. Change is good. Plurality is a reality. My projects at some level always involve manipulation, transformation or even mutation of a given programme to address the future and thereby to achieve a rich, complex and polychromatic architecture which can adapt beyond its decipherable order. Each building is fragmented in a programmatic, spatial and visual sense. These fragments oppose, collide, meet, join, and eventually reconcile themselves into a tense balance of coexistence. The com-plexity thus achieved is of a spatial nature, not necessarily comprising only of a visual juxtaposition of objects. The controlled penetration of the sun and the elements into these volumetric intersection adds another dimension to the spatial complexity.

My attitude towards change response towards external and internal impetus. It is not towards a defined pre-determined goal, but a constant and continuous evaluation of that which is immediately relevant. I view every project as a clean slate to start afresh with the accumulative knowledge of previous designs. Beginning from scratch every time, from door handles to large components, is an additive, perhaps also a subtractive process, a compilation of parts to form the whole. Every completed building a stepping stone to a better understanding of space, intent and context.

The realisation of any architecture is through its construction. To me fabrication is almost an end in itself. I am fortunate to be practising in Indonesia with its tradition of craftsmanship and I try to exploit this potential in all my buildings. Architecture today has a lot to learn from the past. The ability to create environmentally responsive buildings and the ethic of quality craftsmanship are specific Indonesian traditions that I try to emulate in my work. On the other hand we should also realise that today's global economy has dramatically changed the way we perceive our society. I believe that the future of architecture in this region lies in the marriage of the merits of the old and the new.

It is on this account that I do not consider myself a purely Indonesian or Asian architect. I happen to practise in Indonesia and that does not preclude me from being able to function in other environments. Architecture has moved beyond the realm of place with the advent of information technology. We are at an age where appropriate techniques of construction and design are available to us on demand. I believe in this internationalisation of architecture as long as it can learn from and coexist with the traditional.

Sardjono Sani

Complexity and Change

Duta Niaga, the "No-Body" House
Jakarta, Indonesia, 1992.

This 400 sqm. house for a modern Indonesian family is located in a residential area in southern Jakarta. The design of the house presents a debate between the old and the new, between tradition and modern life. Do traditional values govern life in today's society and how do they affect it?

The design strategy was to take two boxes of 8 x 15 m grid with traditional pitched roofs, then project the 'bad' *FengShui* from the T-junction where it is situated as a force into the building. The resulting fracture manifests itself in the design in the form of a shifted construction grid and broken roof forms. The new grid generated by this 'force' is skewed at an angle of 6 degrees from the original grid that governs the house. The 'problem' of the 'bad' *FengShui* was a more important consideration than the internal organisation. This "No-Body" house was designed with no particular individual's programme in mind but is valid for anybody living on that specific site. It allows itself to be affected by tradition and yet challenges it in the context of modern reality.

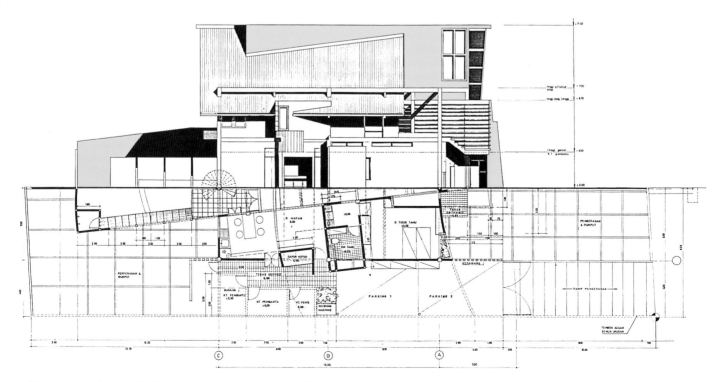

Above and opposite: Longitudinal sections through the long axis of the house

View from street exterior

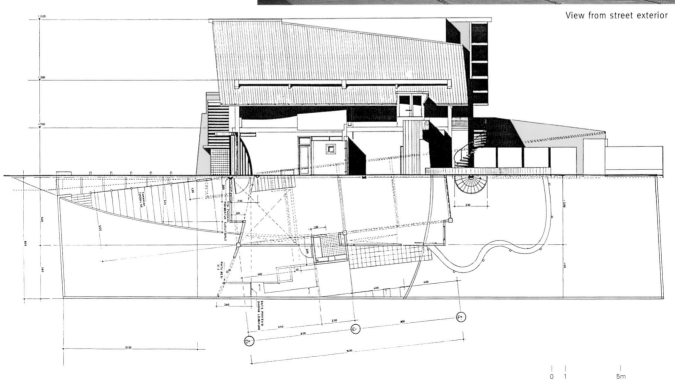

Complex geometries ordering the architectural elements
in the interior

The skewed 'fault line' through the house is articulated as a split
in the roof form

View from pool deck

Kartika House
Jakarta, Indonesia, 1994.

The house is located on a regular plot in a suburb of Jakarta. It is a house that accepts its existence as part of an urban street of row houses; the facade is flat and it turns inside for its definition. Pure, white tectonic volumes produced by the programme intersect and are set in motion by a centrally located double helical staircase. This turbulence impacts onto adjacent walls and sends vibrations into the surrounding volumes. Complex internal transformations are achieved in this way.

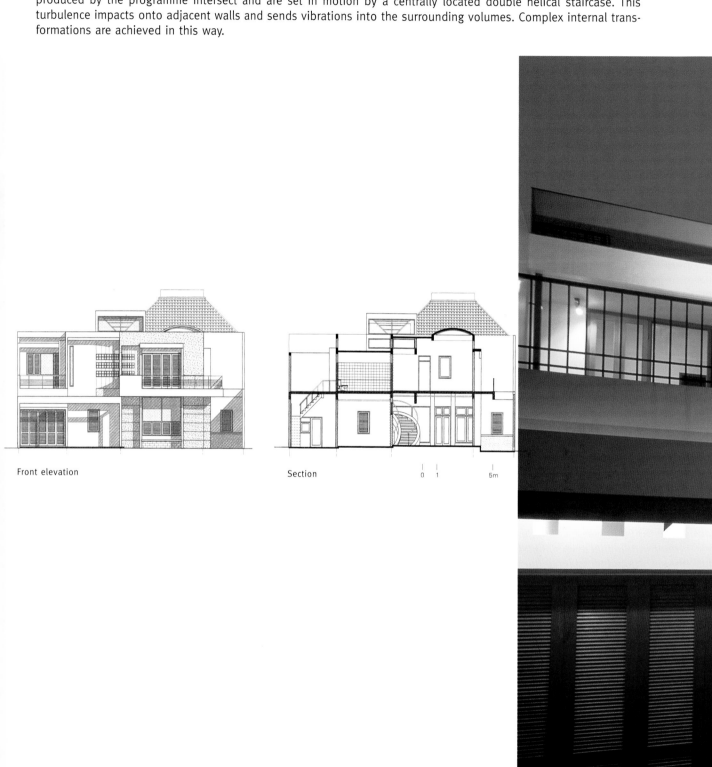

Front elevation

Section

0   1   5m

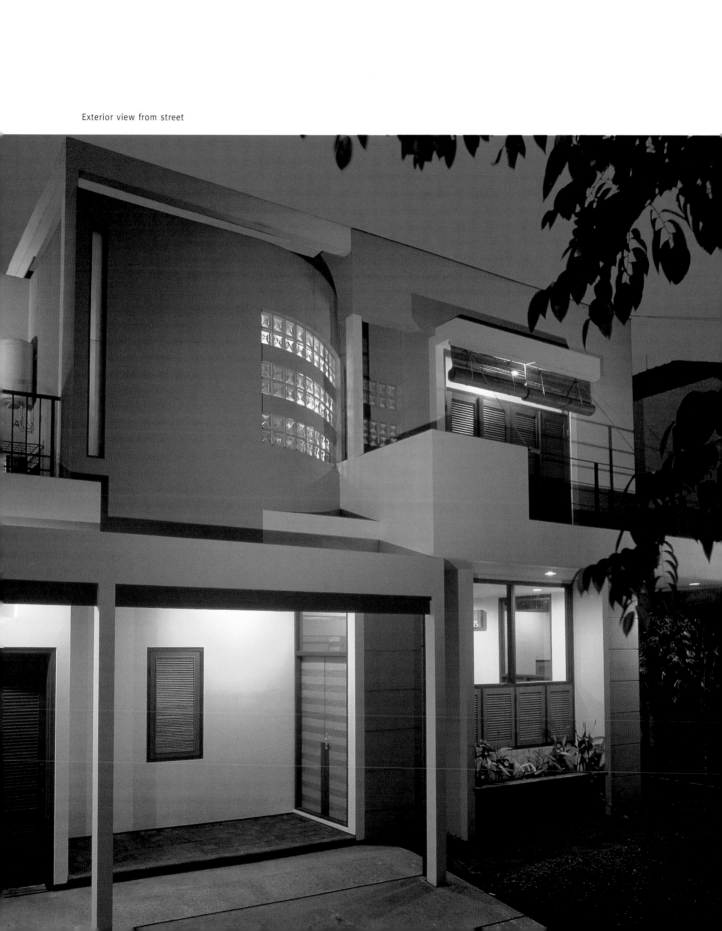

Exterior view from street

First storey plan

Second storey plan

0   1   5m

The double-helical staircase that generates the order of the interior space

Cengkareng House
Jakarta. Indonesia. 1997.

This house in a Jakarta suburb was designed for an architect friend who is a 'strict' modernist. The house is almost completely open with interconnected internal spaces. Excellent cross-ventilation and light characterise each room. The house begins and is resolved from the inside; the external is only a by-product of this exercise. The generated volumes are purely negative; volumes are carved out of an imaginary mass, with the resultant intersections forming the circulation and physical substance of the house. The complexity of the spaces is also reflected in the detailing of each joint. Each joint celebrates the diversity of materials and surfaces used.

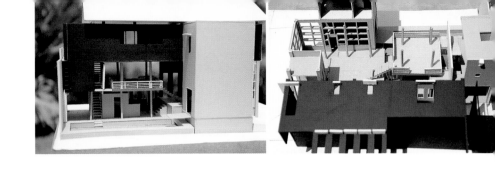

The mezzanine level is articulated as a discreet platform in a large interior volume

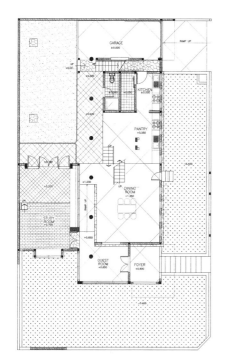

First storey plan

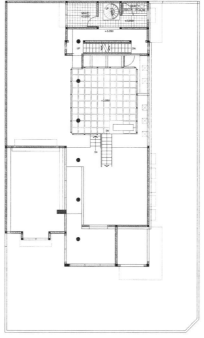

Mezzanine plan

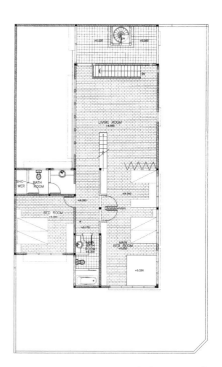

Second storey plan

0   1   5m

Front elevation

Side elevation

0   1   5m

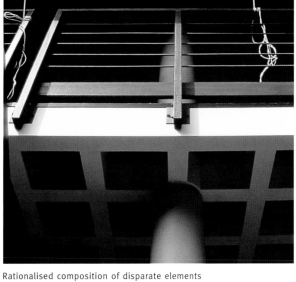

Rationalised composition of disparate elements

Rear courtyard looking towards the study with master
bathroom above

133

All these years have been a long and rather unusual journey. The drops which coalesced at the source gradually became a spring, then a river and now a part of many rivers. In the process of this journey, many lands were traversed, some open and some controlled.

There were moments when the flow ebbed, even stopped, but the stagnation gave rise to a lake. Then the floods overpowered the embankments and pulled me out of the slumber.

The journey saw many lands, forests and gardens over many seasons. In the process, the river drank the water sanctified by great visionaries and the water began to raise questions. The muddy waters began to clear and the journey finally found its path.

Though still not clear, there is a path and pulling strong because deep within, the silent waves of the ocean are heard. It appears that the vast ocean has much to say to the river and the drops which have come a long way.

Everything is interrelated. From the design of a pin to the design of a metropolis. All that one needs to understand is the difference in their scales and their sphere of impacts.

I also realise that even though each object, issue and design should have its own identity, it cannot be conceived in isolation since identity is a mere comparison with what is immediately around and very often this perception is short sighted. All choices of technologies or materials or functions should be born out of their own nature and needs. Their own evolution gives them a character and demonstrates to us their purposes or uses. Hence what we need to do is to allow the purpose of existence to find its relatedness or application.

Time or style likewise is a limited notion. It can easily be set aside if we realise that all that we are presently perceiving is through our memories of past and present, and that there are layers which must be seen together and not as fragmented issues be they of art, architecture or life. It is therefore essential that we look from a distance with eternity or timelessness as the basis so that our solutions are holistic and enduring.

Balkrishna Doshi

Conversation with Doshi

excerpts from a conversation between Balkrishna Doshi and the students and staff of Sangath, Ahmedabad

Architect's Own House
Ahmedabad, India, 1961 (phase 1), 1990 (phase 2)

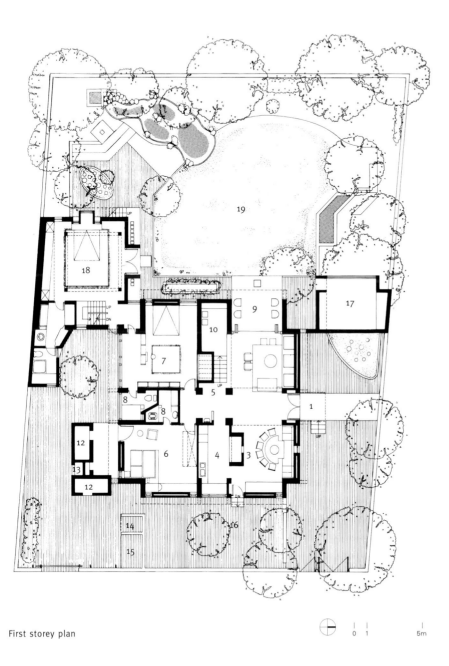

First storey plan

1	Entrance
2	Living room
3	Dining room
4	Kitchen
5	Staircase
6	Children's bedroom
7	Master bedroom
8	Toilet
9	Verandah
10	Music room
11	Pond
12	Servant's room
13	W.C.
14	Pump room
15	Wash
16	Kitchen yard
17	Studio
18	Guest room
19	Garden

0 1   5m

Q: Please tell us about your background and how that has helped you to interpret and understand the nature of Indian society.

I was born in a large extended Hindu family where sharing, respect for varied views and accommodation to unexpected changes was the norm.

From my daily experiences in India, I realised that our society is like a kaleidoscope. Despite the use of the same elements, with every little twist, we constantly multiply images manifold and create patterns that seem strange to us and outsiders in India at first glance but gradually become part of our culture.

First storey guest room

Even an apparent inconsistency is often subjugated by an experiential consistency, and it is this that gives India a diverse, multi-faceted richness which is never provided by a direct, linear experience. Because of these paradoxical situations, stories and myths emerge and are sustained. They become part of our daily life. In them we see our associations and our memories.

Consequently, our experiences are constantly modified, sometimes with no rational justification. They remain our major influences and are directly related to the deeper emotions of our everyday life. Unconsciously they influence us in interpreting the meaning of each space, each form, each expression, be it architectural, artistic or literary.

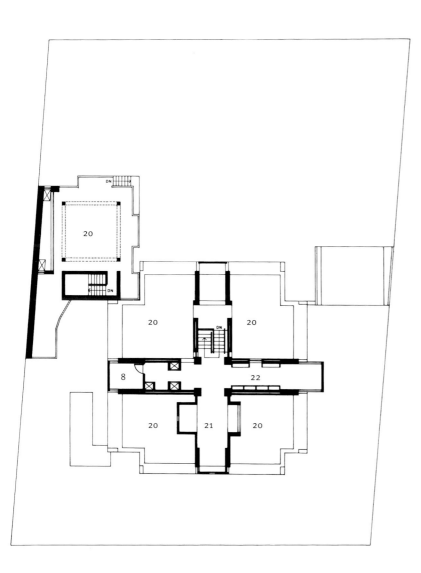

20   20

8

22

20   21   20

20 Open terrace
21 Study room
22 Library

Second storey plan

0 1   5m

In our tradition-bound and plural society, the past still dominates. Our future is enmeshed with it and the paradoxes of presen realities are readily accepted, be they of language, class, caste, or economic in nature. They all seem to thrive in a continuous dynamic relationship. As a result, the known and unknown counter-points which appear paradoxical become highlights in our daily life. This capacity to absorb and assimilate a "homogeneous heterogeneity" is what I regard as the true strength of our culture.

East elevation

0 1   5m

Q: In what way would you say the nature of Indian society has influenced its architecture?

In our architecture, the void, the silence, the distance, the emotions always generate a tenuous or perhaps a strong relationship within all the elements that constitute our daily life. They all offer us multiple concepts of celebration of life suitable to each individual. For example the architecture of classical temples, or the humble mud houses of the desert villages, or even the traditional inner city houses and street structures where immense alternatives and symbols are created out of similar elements both timeless and the time-bound can be mentioned.

Husain-Doshi Gufa
Ahmedabad. India. 1993.

In such architecture, when you look at the plan, you can discover a lattice that simultaneously holds it together which is permeable allowing movement which is multi-dimensional. The alternative routes are as clear as the main one yet they are related to one another in such a manner that none of these can be dropped. One can easily shift from the main route to the sub-route, sub-route to the main route or use only one route throughout. This choice of routing is very important because in this movement the sense of time is modified. subsequently the space gets modified and perception begins to change.

The South Indian temples or cities like Jaipur are fine examples of this. They allow one to go at his or her desired pace and feel, not only the *axis mundi*, but also a sense of being directed there because of the three dimensional hierarchy that is built in the lattice. This is another essential component of such a concept that does not push but make one directly and instinctively aware of his or her position vis-à-vis the immediate world and the associational or the mythical world.

For example, a Hindu temple tells you of a certain order but does this subtly and joyfully. As a result one accepts it; without being compelled. This issue of choice is very important in architecture. One must have choices and indirect suggestions. One should only be guided.

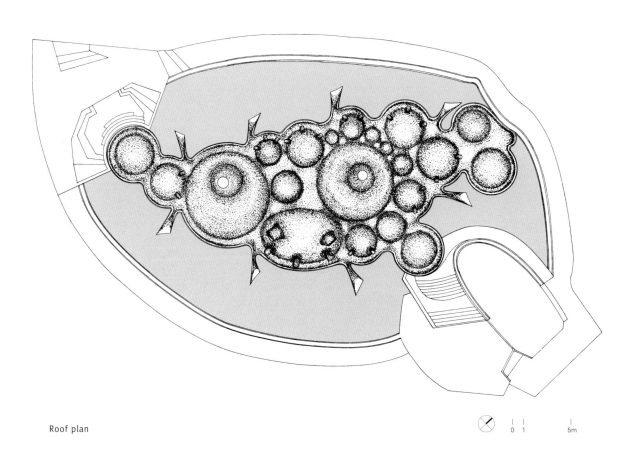

Roof plan

0 1   5m

There is a focus in Indian architecture but it is not concentric. It meanders, expands like an octopus. The boundary acts as a buffe[r]
and enmeshes the areas where things happen based on the kind of usage and their relation to the centre and the periphery. Thu[s]
even the periphery becomes as important as the centre.

Our architecture is concerned with the behaviour patterns and the rituals, that is, the question of prerogative, order, frame, peripher[y]
and centre. The way this is conveyed is that while a system exists it is not the ultimate since time is not in our hands, neither th[e]
choices that the future provides.

Sections

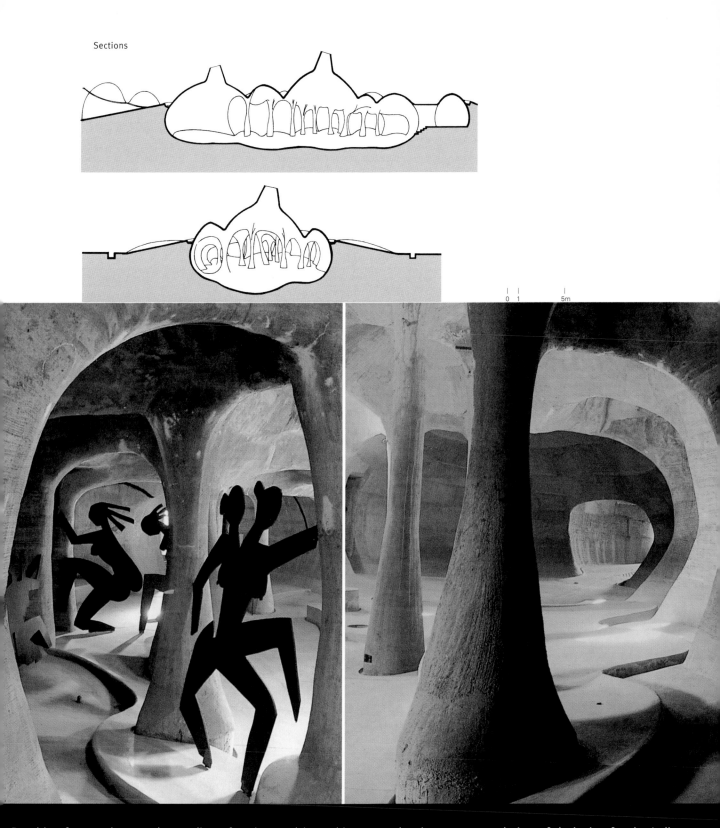

| | 0 | 1 | 5m |

: Resulting from such an understanding of society and its architecture, what is your personal view of designing for the Indian ontext?

often wonder which context is true? The world that I dream of or the one I have lived in? Which period of locational architecture and t is true – the old or the unknown? Can creativity be achieved by employing familiar idioms or the unfamiliar? I believe, it is in the rsuit of the unfamiliar that one has just discovered and whose final result makes your heart throb and brings about a wholeness

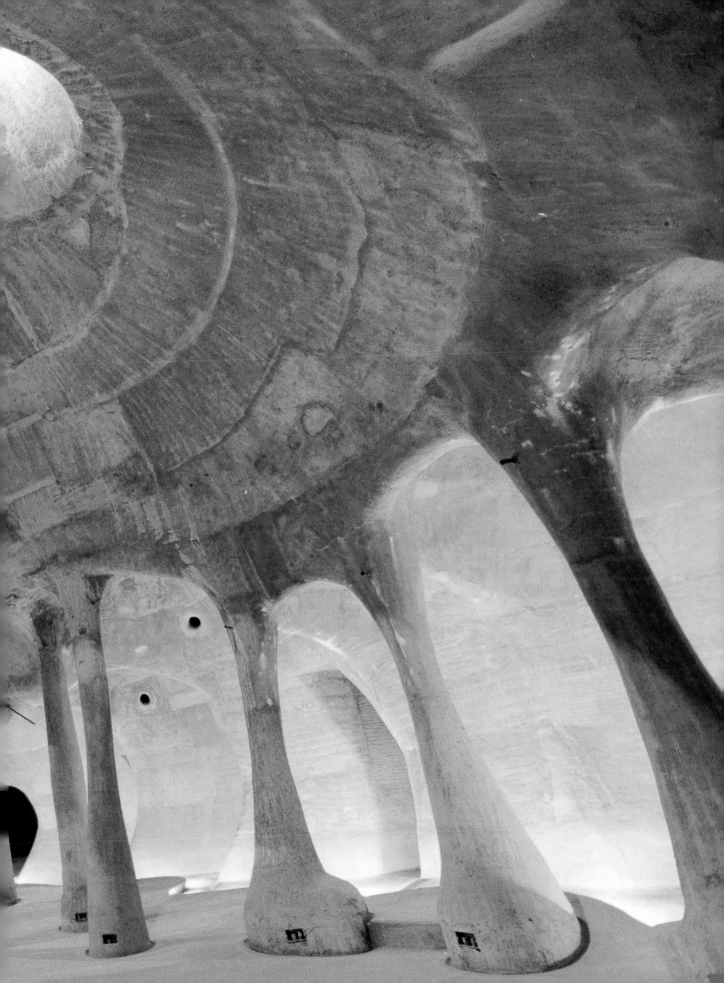

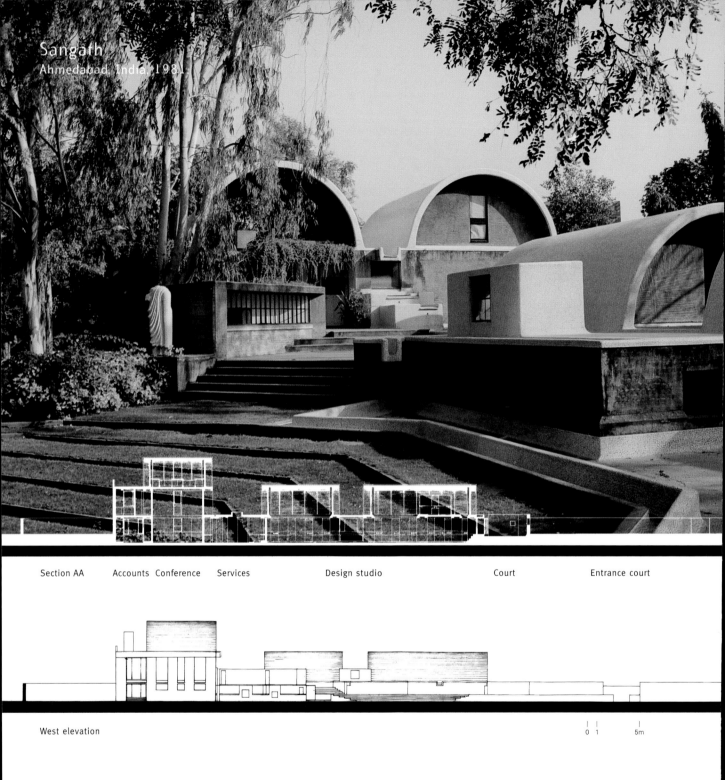

Sangath
Ahmedabad, India, 1981

Section AA   Accounts   Conference   Services   Design studio   Court   Entrance court

West elevation

0   1   5m

The dilemma that I face every day is having to constantly experience the living traditions. I am almost hypnotised by the mixture of past, present, and a hint of the future experienced through travels and the television. When we are too preoccupied with the past it becomes a 'hook' to hold on to. It is comfortable to be with yesterday which is known and predictable. To accept the present, that is today, as it is, one has to answer questions: what is that which is valid or what will this offer to our grandchildren which can help us all grow and nourish? The real challenge is to become simultaneous, take the past, the present and the future as continuous and tie it to our aspirations.

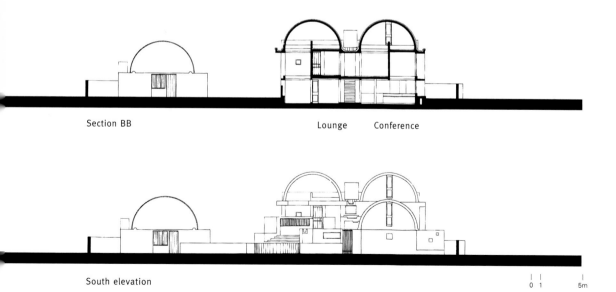

Section BB   Lounge   Conference

South elevation   0 1   5m

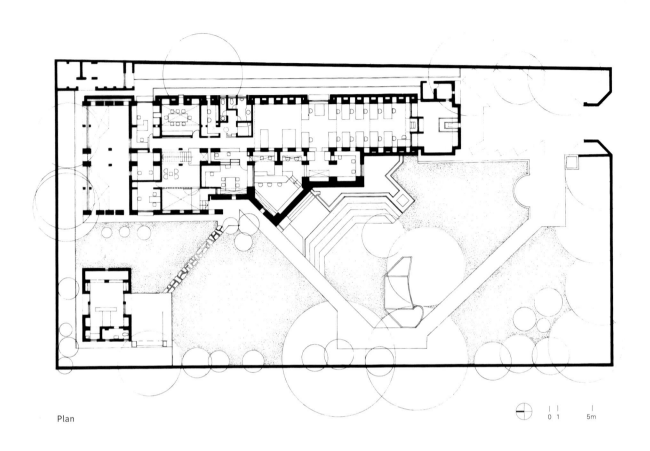

Plan

⊕ | | |
   0 1   5m

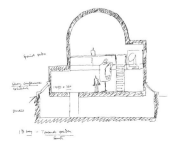

Aranya Community Housing
Indore, India, 1986.

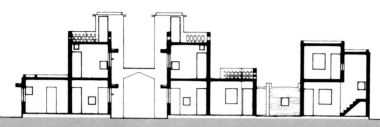

Q: How did you take up the task of pioneering modern architectural education in India?

I am convinced that an architect and a designer has a much larger role to play in the community and in society than what he does today.

He should not just be a vehicle for the expression of different attitudes; he must be, through his skill and ingenuity, a builder of attitudes also. He must be the agent to inculcate amongst all an attitude to live with others, rather than simply consolidate only the attitude to live. His designs must have a place for everybody and must offer everyone a role in the process of building the total environment.

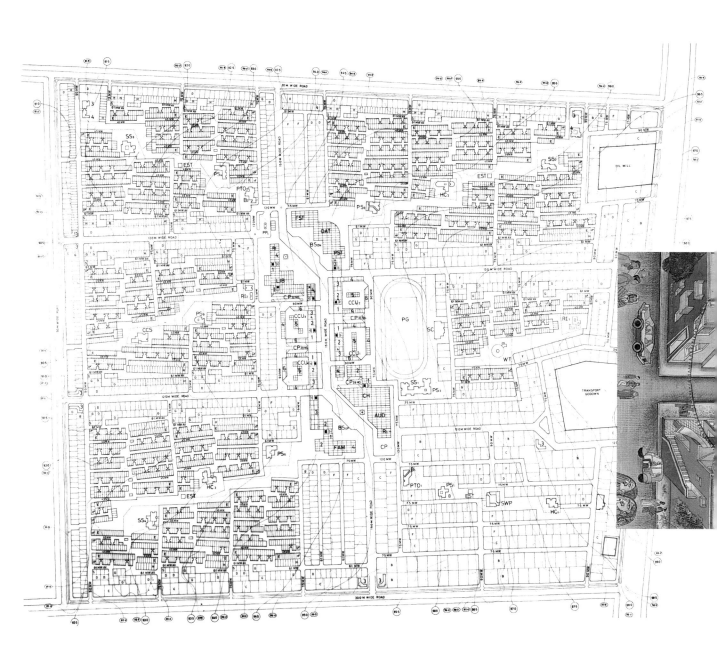

That is why I believe that an architect and a designer must put the highest emphasis on communal and social institutions, becaus
there is no better tool than this for creating an attitude for total living. History has taught us this lesson, and the growing disintegra-
tion of society today is the result of breaking away from institutions. We must revive them.

We must bring institutions back to the forefront. And we must in due course put them back as the focal points of design if w
want society and the community to continue their advancement in such a way that everybody is given his or her share of th

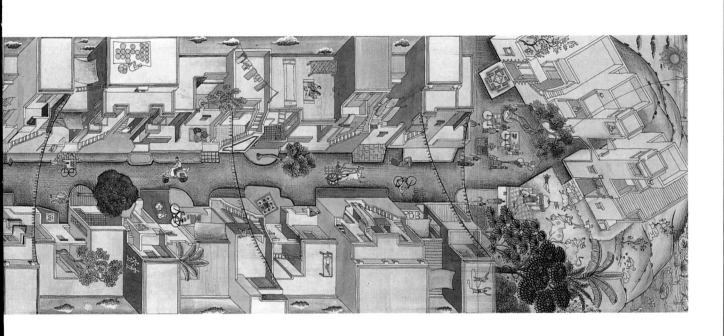

Q: Some of your recent works in the last decade or so are marked by a tremendous change compared to earlier projects. How is your new understanding of your contexts translated in design?

When I returned from Paris and set up my practice at Ahmedabad my work was certainly influenced by my experiences of working with Corbusier. However my collaboration with Louis I Kahn on the Indian Institute of Management, Ahmedabad project began a process of requestioning my beliefs and a fresh discovery of my contexts, more of the metaphysical nature. Corbusier, in projects like the Chapel at Ronchamp and Kahn in almost all his work, were discovering new horizons of architecture unfettered by a dogmatic Modernism. A pursuit of pure creativity, more intuitive in nature and less rational.

Bharat Diamond Bourse

Mumbai, India (ongoing 1999).

Section

I, for my part, began to discover the experiential aspects of Indian towns and cities. I became aware of the dynamic qualities and th manner in which forms became formless with the ultimate form being the experience itself. I became conscious about the built an the unbuilt spaces, the solids and the voids which meet through the skin that we call architecture. I also became conscious of th enduring values of architecture which need not be directed at the immediate but towards values which are timeless and which endur for centuries. In such architecture, past, present and future are all one.

Then only the spaces, both solid and void, of our architecture emanate an energy which makes architecture vibrant, throbbing wit life, as if it were a living being celebrating every act of life. This is what I am trying to discover in my recent projects.

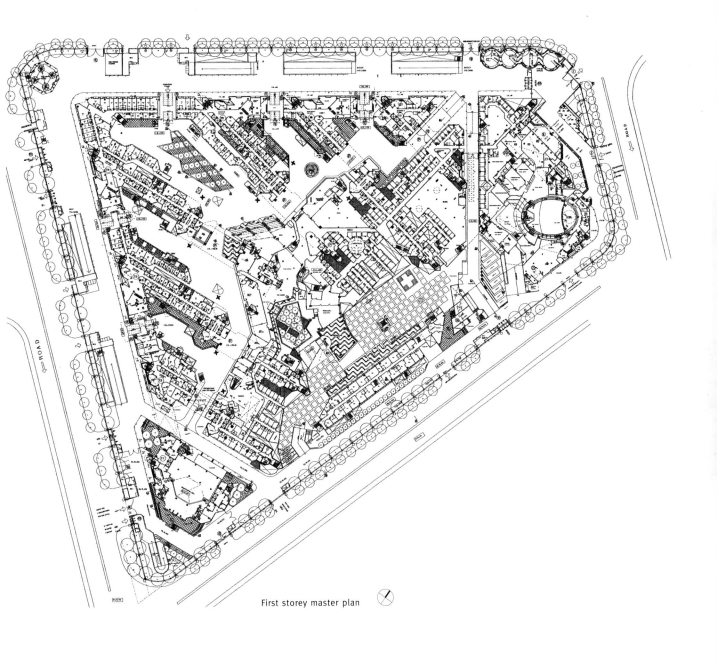

First storey master plan

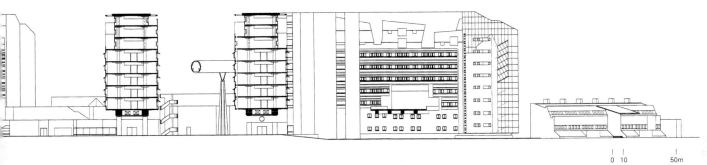

0 10   50m

What I like (or dislike)

The roof is a very important visual and practical element in Southeast Asian architecture. The horizontal line always creates a magical touch to forms that play with it.

I try to achieve the right image for the place.
I like images that come from a specific place and a specific cultural heritage, not generic images.
I like to avoid generic form, form that is too clean and lacks touches of local cultural heritage.
I love pure forms, comfortable and visually organised planning with good three-dimensional proportions.
I try to arrive at a clear and decisive form and how functions should be arranged.

I conceptualise on three scales: planning, architecture, and interior at the same time during the design process.
I like to break forms down and express them into "master" spaces and "servant" spaces. A clear expression of Form - this is what I learnt from Kahn's work.
I like to use wood, cement and glass as basic materials.
I always try to preserve and enhance existing land, water and trees as much as I can.

A real tropical feeling is a must.

I like high pitched roofs.
I like a strong geometry both in plan and in three-dimensional form.
I like a dramatic skyline; a combination of "roofscape" and "treescape".
I always attempt to break scale down.
I don't believe monumentality has anything to do with scale.
I like pavilions rather than a large mass.
I like visual penetration through building to the sky, trees and beyond.

I like understated architecture, I expect landscape to create surprises and camouflage and shade the building.

I like to see the paddy fields hiding behind a dense group of trees because it creates a sense of visual expectation.
I like to turn before entering a building.
I like courtyards; I like buildings that form open space.
I like repetitions because they can create light and shadows that in turn create a stillness in us.

In a building, I like to reduce the types of architectural languages as much as possible and use them to create variety.

I like buildings which are buildable by local people without the need for imported high technology.

I love the early morning and late evening sun because they give long soft shadows without any glare.
I don't like glare - it hurts my eyes, that's why I need a hat.
I like Malay and Thai fascia boards because they make friends with sunlight.
I love continuous breeze when I am in a room, or under a tree.
I like to make rooms which invite breeze to come and go.
If I can, I would like to build without any glass but having a very cool inside by way of bringing water elements deep into the building.
I love connectors between forms because I think beauty lies there.

I love to treat both rain and sunshine as friends.

I have no fear of decorative elements.
I like the decorative elements in traditional Thai architecture.
I love the Thai house. I like the superb organisation of
traditional Japanese architecture.
I like Katsura.
I like the completeness of language and
beauty of traditional Balinese architecture.
I like the pure structure of traditional Javanese architecture.
I like the lightness of form and intense expression of the decorative
elements in traditional Burmese architecture.
I like the solitude of old temple settings in northern Thailand.
I like the simple and sincere architecture of temples in the
countryside of Thailand.

I like trees with strong and defined forms.
I don't like buildings to appear as if they just jumped out from
the surrounding landscape.
I like them to be obscure and shaded by trees (in front, behind and in between).

I like buildings to be lower than trees.
I don't like to see the sky and the roof ridge, rather,
I like to see the sky, trees, then the roof ridge below.

I like finials because they make the roof appear lighter and
tell us that it is Thai or Burmese.

I like the fun of borrowing forms from Burma to put in Thailand and vice versa
because we have been doing this all through our history.
I like to borrow Javanese Pendopol (a pure and perfect square plan) and
combine it with the beautiful Malay porch.

In my architecture, I hope to achieve two things:
it must be *unmistakably* Thai, Javanese, Burmese, etc.
and it must belong to our time with the modern comforts of today.

I hope in future to create architecture with more quality of stillness,
solitude and surprise just like the ancient Sukhothai Wat Tonquen
in northern Thailand.

I hope to extend our Southeast Asian cultural heritage f u r t h e r.

Baiyoke-Kandawgyi Hotel, Yangon Myanmar, 1996. In collaboration with Bensley Design Studios.

Baiyoke-Kandawgyi Hotel

Baiyoke-Kandawgyi Hotel

Baiyoke-Kandawgyi Hotel

Baiyoke-Kandawgyi Hotel

Regent Chiangmai Resort, Chiengmai, Thailand, 1996. (1996 Conservation Award by Siamese Institute of Architects.)   In collaboration with Bensley Design Studios.

Regent Chiengmai Resort

Regent Chiengmai Resort

Novotel Lombok, Lombok, Indonesia, 1997.

Novotel Lombok

Novotel Lombok

Pangkor Laut Resort, Lumut, Malaysia, 1993. (Nominated for Aga Khan Award.) In collaboration with Bensley Design Studios.

Pangkor Laut Resort

Pangkor Laut Resort

My 1986 dissertation at Harvard Graduate School of Design explored the issue of spatial transformation, focusing on the transition from tradition to modernity. The study looked at elements of behaviour, pattern, and the essential qualities that have remained in urban space over the centuries. Textural material was drawn from the Sung dynasty "Scroll Drawing" by Chang Tse-Duan. The pedestrian zone of Taipei's downtown central business district provided a contemporary site model. Both paradigms transform, decipher, and redefine an urban spatial structure that transcend differences of time and place through the abstracted and defunctionalised process of *deconstruction* and *reorganisation*. The importance of this process is that it lends greater legibility to urban space. It is also useful in formulating architectural strategies aimed at Taiwan's commercialised, superficial, and ephemeral urban space. In addition, I hope to go beyond conventional thinking about modernisation of tradition. Taiwan's urban fabric suffers from an over intermingling of publicity and privacy, monumentality and transience. Clarifying and defining a hierarchical spatial structure in this confusion is a central issue of urbanism throughout Asia.

Hu Shyr-Fong

Layered Clarity

Temporary Architecture:
Sales Reception Centres
Hsichih and Neihu, Taiwan, 1996-1997.

Reception centres for the sale of property developments are a unique phenomenon in Taiwan's real estate industry. Serving as an *in situ* space for the transaction of property, these buildings are simple in design and built for temporary use, typically three to six months. Ironically it is this transient nature that allows greater latitude for defining their image than would be possible in more permanent buildings. The centres follow the same general principles in terms of layout. Every effort is made to orient the front facade to the main street and to give an impression of size.

The interior space is usually divided into a central sales area and adjacent areas for the display of architectural models and show units. The Hsichih project makes use of a 25-metre corridor to delineate a viewing path. This walkway in turn articulates the main facade. In the Neihu project, the model display area is centrally placed, imparting monumentality to the overall space and heightening the plasticity of the facade. Construction and detailing of these projects are standardised whenever possible to shorten the construction time and to reduce cost. Planes and facades are scaled to accommodate standard 60 x 240 cm plywood panels. Doorways, windows, ceilings, and even air-conditioning units are designed to fit this standard module. Courtyards, an extension of the building's exterior, are generally geometrically arranged. Asphalt is the material of choice due to its low cost, with texture and linear patterns provided by wood strips. These elements give the courtyards their clean feel and are durable enough to handle the centres' heavy pedestrian traffic.

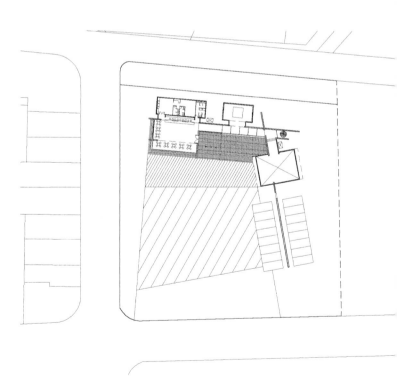

Temporary architecture 1: Sales reception centre at Hsichih

Below: A 25-m long corridor delineates a viewing path

Temporary architecture 2: The plasticity of facade of the sales reception centre at Neihu

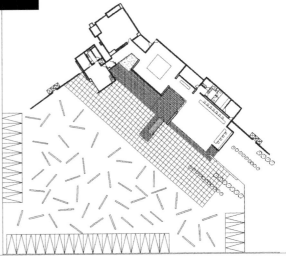

Temporary Architecture 2: Sales reception centre at Neihu

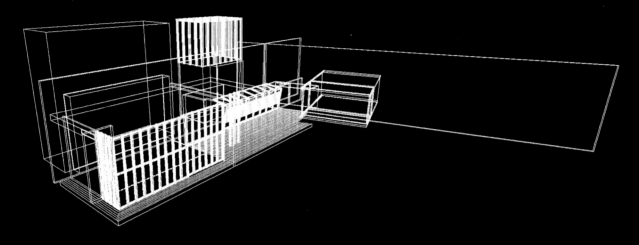

Temporary Architecture 1

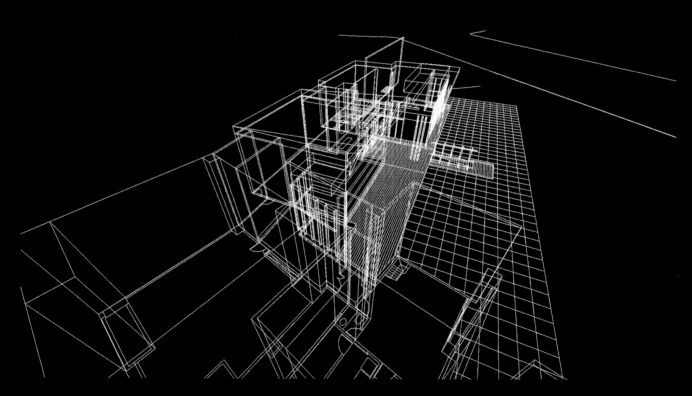

Temporary Architecture 2

Furniture Design
1993.

My furniture design
is an extension
of my conception of
architectural space.
It explores the
relationship between
light and space and
tries to achieve a
dynamic balance.

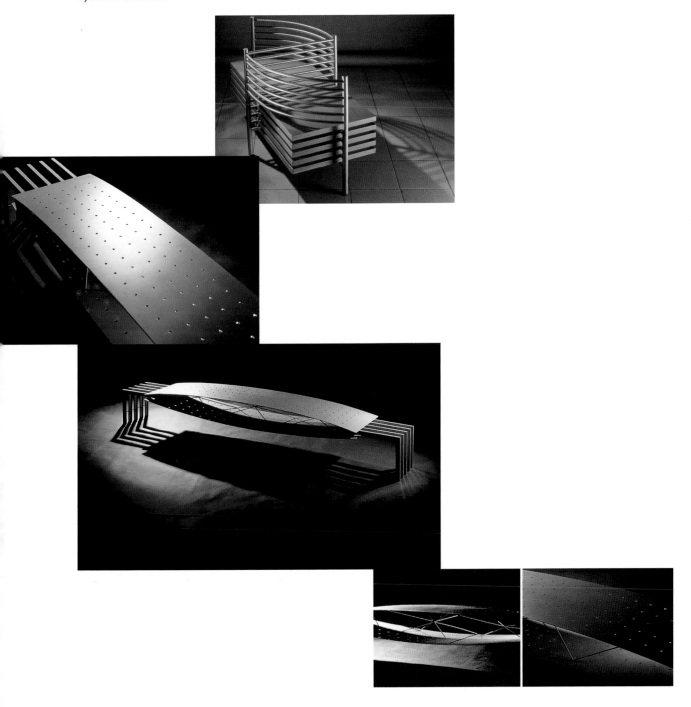

Hillside Residence.
Taipei, Taiwan, 1996.

This building is located
at a chasm of a hill.
The chasm was the result
of poor real estate
planning which left a
vertical slope sprayed
with light-weight concrete
at the back of the
building after some
excavation. The apart-
ment follows a U-shaped
plan with the residual
space facing this
wounded hill. Rather
than hiding this space,
I decided to exploit its
potential and in the
process create a more
varied living environment.
I wanted to infuse the
space with a positive
"sense" with walls facing
this "voided" space
replaced by glass sliding
doors. This composition
of a half-open, multi-
layered exterior diffuses
the inside/outside
boundaries hence making
the "void" an extension
of the interior space.

The U-shaped configuration facing the 'wounded' hill

Plan

Opposite: The kitchen and service zone is given an additional layer of privacy with the use of a timber screen

Looking back at the house with its multiple layers of translucencies

Architect's Own House
Taichung. Taiwan. 1995.

The design for my home evolved as a prototype of the ideal house rather than as a concept based on a specific interior plan. I started by making the elevation modular with I-beams placed at 130 cm intervals. Fenestration consisted of fixed and operable windows and timber louvres. Through a rich layering of different materials, I sought to create a highly textured effect that defines levels of privacy. At the same time I hope to endow transitional spaces with a sense of ambiguity and suspense.

The hidden bathroom adjacent to the main space

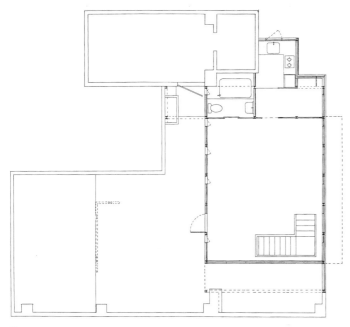

Plan

Unity of structure and space is emphasised in this one-volume house

Man must build to complement and to preserve the balance, the "yin yang" of the land.

Man is only temporal. The structures he builds outlast him.

The built environment is established; it is the establishment. The establishment has much more prevailing rights.

The newcomer must in humility succumb to that which is already there; he must complement it.

In the architectural world there is no such situation where ideal conditions become available to the architect. He has to make the "ideal" condition happen. One has to seize opportunities as they come and turn disadvantage into advantage.

The wholesale importation of ideas and icons from the West is too silly to be acceptable.

To set a new direction for Asian architects and to give those who live in the tropics a sense of pride in their work and relishing their difference from the West, that is one of my objectives.

I think "Asian urbanism" is a dirty word.
Most of the Malaysian cities and towns do not have large spaces or walking streets for the people to enjoy.
Therefore, where is the value or distinctiveness of Asian urbanism?

Jimmy C. S. Lim

The Rites of the Tropics

My approach to architectural design is simple: understand your context to create the architecture that is suitable for the environment that you live in; understand the place, where you are, who you are. There are two aspects of architecture that influence my thinking as an architect. One is what I term "Architecture of Humility" and the other, the "Tai-Chi" of Architecture. When I talk about humility I am referring to the suppression of one's ego in the face of the situation, and how it wants to be resolved.

The Architecture of Humility

Humility Towards Nature

My contention has always been that you must be humble towards Nature, respect her and see her do wonders for you. The Chinese call this aspect of respecting nature "Feng Shui", translated as "Wind, Water". "Feng Shui" is nothing mysterious. It merely means studying a site in its natural state and using that knowledge to design. Vitruvius mentioned this in his *Ten Books on Architecture*. You need to understand where the prevailing winds are coming from, where the sunrise and where the sunset is; how rain and surface-water run-offs behave; and the implications of possible underground water movement and the direction of its flow. The other very vital aspect totally related to the spiritual is the aspect of the site. The most important and pleasant view must take prominence. This is the aspect that will provide the most stimulation to your spiritual self.

Nature is balance; it is the perfect "yin yang". The interdependence and interaction of all natural things as an order is most obvious in nature. You need only to look at any ecosystem, however small, to realise that the factors present interact to produce a system so stable it is able to sustain itself over a long period. Within that entity everything works. On a macro scale, then, you need to look and survey the natural surroundings. Try to understand what nature has provided you, what it wants to be and not what you want it to be. Man must build to complement and to preserve the balance, the "yin yang" of the land. It makes no sense to upset the perfect order that exists in nature, rather, take advantage of its bounty by 'going along with it', so to speak. To do this we must humble ourselves first, then take a closer look at nature and try to understand it. Nature is a benevolent teacher.

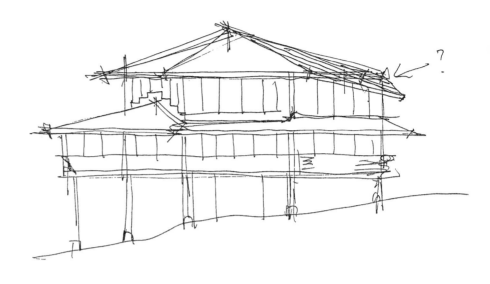

Humility Towards History, Tradition and the Built Environment

"Welcome ladies and gentlemen, welcome to Suzhou. Suzhou is an ancient city and this year we shall be celebrating our 25th Century."

This was the tour guide's welcome that greeted the PAM (Malaysian Institute of Architects) delegates when they visited Suzhou in China in 1986. 25th Century! That works out to be 2,500 years – the mind cannot perceive this length of time, it is beyond comprehension. What is amazing is that there still are structures built 25 centuries ago – the pagodas, the canal network all the way to Xian and Beijing. It humbles you. It makes you realise how infinitely small man is in time. The people are long gone but their deeds, their built structures – the built environment – still stand as testimony to their wealth, richness of culture and architecture. Seeing Suzhou reminded me of Ercolano outside Naples, except that in the latter case it was a silent, sad and tragic yet imposing testimony of what the former built environment must have been. Both examples carry one message: Man is only temporal. The structures he builds outlast him. What a wealth of information is left to us from ages gone by.

In building to last, the architect must humble himself to the built environment which has been around much longer. I feel that in humility to the built environment, he must try to organise and build accordingly. The built environment is established; it is the establishment. The establishment has much more prevailing rights. The newcomer must in humility succumb to that which is already there; he must complement it. The end result is a totality of the built environment.

Humility Towards Mankind

The problem surrounding mankind is too great for one to even conceive. To think that one is able to solve some of the world's problems is certainly most presumptuous. At best one can try to understand human nature and behaviour. You have to look at the problems of mankind and be sympathetic. This realisation hopefully can help the architect solve some of the related architectural problems. Mankind is made up of many heterogeneous groups where the texture and quality of life are different. In venturing forth, the architect must approach the situation cautiously and with humility.

Humility is nothing new in the context of our Malaysian social fabric. The traditional Chinese and Malay cultures emphasise humility and softness of approach. Therefore "softly, softly" is a virtue to be cultivated.

The "Tai-Chi" of Architecture

Turning a disadvantage into an advantage is to capitalise on the foreign force with which you are up against; this is borrowed from the art of "tai-chi" – a form of "kung-fu" fighting. It utilises the strength of the opponent to overwhelm him.

In the architectural world there is no such situation where ideal conditions become available to the architect. He has to make the "ideal" condition happen. One has to seize opportunities as they come and turn disadvantage into advantage. It is like surfing – your advantage lies in riding with the wave; go against it and you will get into trouble. When a horse is travelling in one direction and you in the other, a head-on collision becomes inevitable, but if you were to jump on its back and ride it, you will be able to direct it, control it and guide it in the direction you want it to go. I use of a lot of timber in the houses I design. This is the result of seeing what has been going on in the Malaysian built environment. The urbanscape in our cities is not something we can be proud of. It is repeating mistakes the West made thirty or forty years ago. Timber is very "Malaysian" and also very traditional. People here tend to look down on timber houses, thinking that only the poor live in them. That is a fallacy. Timber houses are not only beautiful and functional, but cheaper and easier to construct and maintain. I sometimes leave the timber untreated or unfinished, to allow it to age with time and the elements; and it ages so beautifully.

The Rites of the Tropics

The tropical climate of Malaysia only has two seasons: "hot and wet", and "hot and wet and more wet".
The tropics is a CELEBRATION of the following.

1

Colours of differing intensity and variation, of shapes and sizes, of the play of light against darkness.

2

Sounds of water, of the rainfall, of the rivers and flowing streams.

Asian Renaissance

This brings up the question of the Asian psyche in general, but the Malaysian in particular. Is the Oriental mental make-up inferior to that of the Occidental? Why are so many Malaysian architectural works copies of American/European models? Do we assume that architects from the hot, humid low-land tropics are incapable of designing good architecture for the future? What is the rationale for the continuous reproduction and perpetualisation of recycled ideas of mediocrity? In this respect, architecture in this region is at the crossroads. The environment is being threatened and the architectural models being created are not things which many Asian architects can be proud of. This is the same sickness, an epidemic, which the whole of Asia suffers from, except perhaps Japan. The wholesale importation of ideas and icons from the West is too silly to be acceptable.

To set a new direction for Asian architects and to give those who live in the tropics a sense of pride in their work and relishing their difference from the West, that is one of my objectives. Too many architects trained in the West have simply regurgitated ideas they have learnt without considering their appropriateness when implementing them back in their homeland. Asian and colonial subservience to Western dominance is so prevalent that it is something that will take time to overcome – perhaps 150 years from now.

An Asian renaissance is needed to set us off to what we want to achieve and it has to be done with the combined effort of Asians pulling together. This is where I hope my work will in some small way contribute towards this cause.

3
Smells of nature, of the ground as heat surrenders itself to the rain, of decay and death as the sun and heat sap the life out of discarded organic matters.

4
It evokes a **processional route** celebrating a **transformation of sensuality** accentuated by the **heat and the humidity.**

5
It enhances a **visual experience** and celebration tantalised by the **different layering of shapes, light and shade, variety of hues** and the **mysticism of the unseen and unanticipated.**

6

Tropical architecture allows a **symbiotic relationship** between **man-made elements and nature, a cerebral relationship laced with emotions and memories.** It embraces totally all of one's senses.

7

It provides the opportunity for the invisible **"structure" of nature** to be "stylised" and **"framed" in the organic expression** of the roof form and other interior parts and structures.

8

The mysticism of **transparency, layering of forms, light, shade, structural texture,**
– accentuates the **visual surrealism of the space**
– blurs the distinction between **space, distance and time.**

The Salinger Residence
Bangi, Malaysia, 1992.

Winner of the 1998 Aga Khan Award for Architecture.
A return to timber.

Top: Seating detail of the
verandah *(anjung)*
Bottom: "Birdsmouth detail"

Section

0 1   5m

History can be...

9
a **juxtapositioning of memories,** focusing on one's vista on the journey of time and history. It **contextualises the visual** composition.

10
a **weaving** of the lattice screens, a **delineation** of the flooring, an **exploding** of the walls, creating depth, transparency and surrealism.

The Precima Residence
Kuala Lumpur, Malaysia, 1988.

A sensitive response to the environment and nature within a tight urban context.

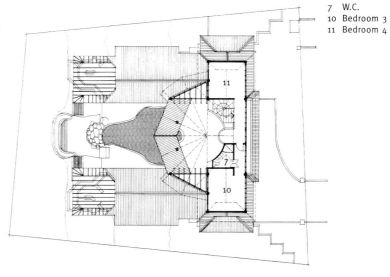

7   W.C.
10 Bedroom 3
11 Bedroom 4

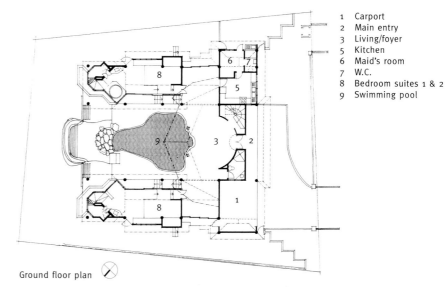

1 Carport
2 Main entry
3 Living/foyer
5 Kitchen
6 Maid's room
7 W.C.
8 Bedroom suites 1 & 2
9 Swimming pool

Ground floor plan

11

an **integrater of structural** elements, **freezing** the integrated complexities of **structures** found in **nature**.

12

Darkness and **shade** intimate **coolness** and act as a **visual magnet** on one's sensitivities, in contrast to the surrounding **brightness** and **heat.**

The magnetism between light and shade is a constant continuing conflict of pain and joy. The tension between light and shade perpetuates the continuing search for comfort and discomfort.

The Schynder Residence
Kuala Lumpur, Malaysia, 1993.

A follow-on of the Precima Residence. Captures the spirit of regional, vernacular and tropical architecture in harmony.

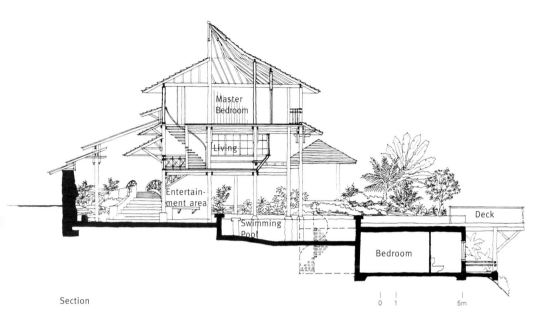

Section

External detail of dining space over pool

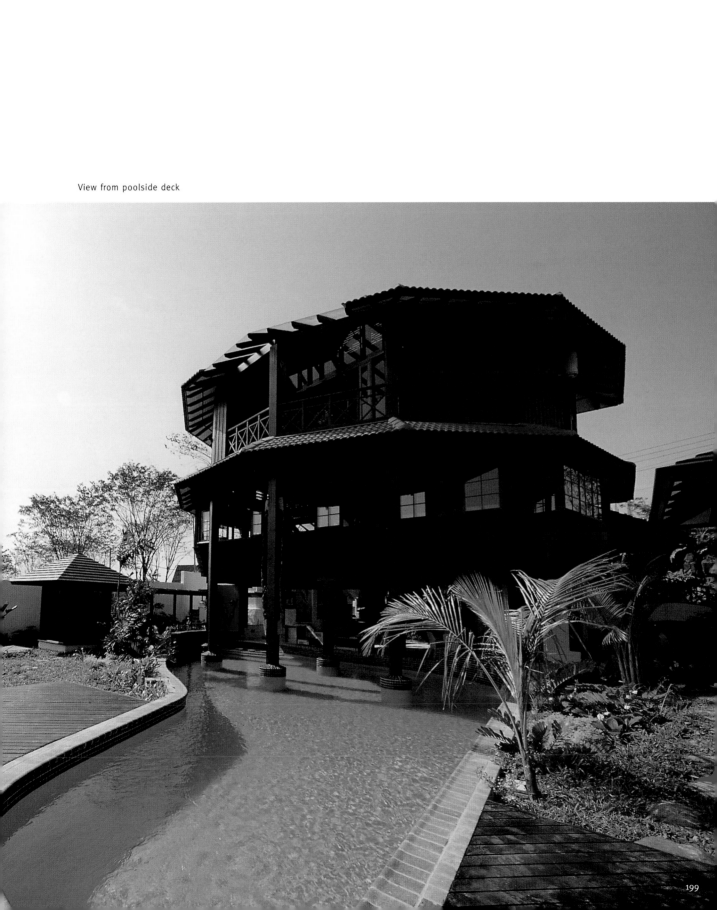

View from poolside deck

The Impiana Beach Resort Cherating
Cherating, Malaysia. 1993.

View from the cooling pool.   *Inset* View from Cherating Beach.

Architect's Own House
Kuala Lumpur, Malaysia (ongoing 1999).

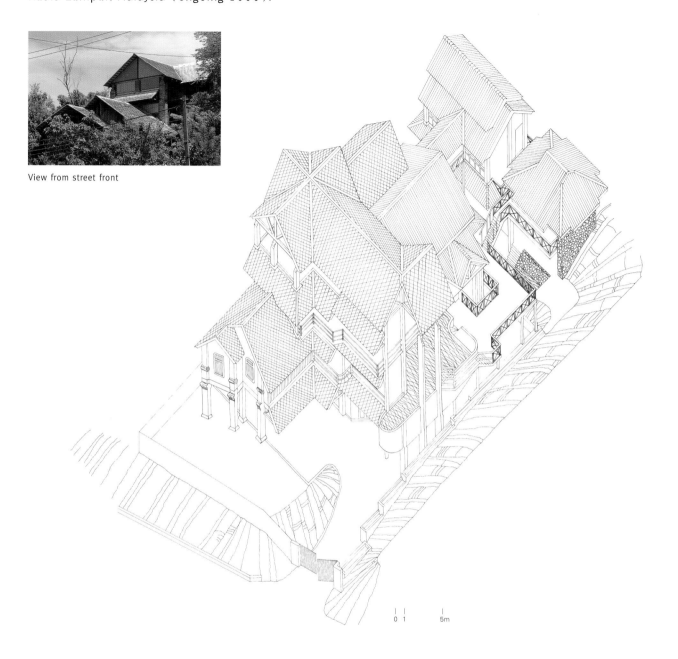

View from street front

0 1	5m

The music pavilion

Detail of breathing walls

Asian Cities

I think "Asian urbanism" is a dirty word. It is dirty because it has degraded all that used to co-exist in an orderly fashion into chaos. It has led to the total destruction of what was a social fabric which bonded people together. The order has been destroyed. This is the result of applying and superimposing urban planning theories onto the Asian context without evaluating their impact. Urban patterns which used to function and contribute towards a lifestyle no longer sustain the urban centres. Most Asian cities, if they can be called cities, only came into being fairly recently. Prior to this these cities were more informal gathering places and centres of commerce. Modern cities in Asia have been taken over by the motorcar. The visual unity and urban pattern have been disrupted by motorways and highways which now criss-cross the urban landscape. Buildings are torn down to make way for these massive motorways. Large sums of money are set aside for expansion of the road network to facilitate traffic flow. The construction of roads has destroyed the fragile urban life which existed before.

Beijing used to be a people-friendly city. Since the opening up of China the motorcar has taken over. Now Beijing is fast becoming a city with nothing more than a gridlock of highways. Even the smaller scaled residential areas are not spared. The streets are choked with cars. Walking streets have but fast disappeared. Other cities in Asia do not even have walking streets. Most of the Malaysian cities and towns do not have large spaces or walking streets for the people to enjoy. Therefore, where is the value or distinctiveness of Asian urbanism? It is a total disregard for that which has existed before. Modern cities and urban centres are being planned and built, adopting Western values and approaches in their layout. It has resulted in an identity crisis because of the similarity to the originals found in the West. There are many urban areas in Singapore and Hong Kong which are pure reproductions of other Western cities.

Burmah Road, Penang, 1972

New coastal road to Bayar Lepas Airport, Penang, 1999

Penang, Northern Road Enclave, 1998

Tropical City

The main preoccupation when designing for the tropics is to keep the sun and rain out; and to allow as much cross-ventilation as possible. These two requirements are, however, contradictory. The sun heats the place up but the rain cools it down. A roof is needed to keep the sun and rain off one's head, but you also need walls to keep the inside of the building cool, shaded from direct sunlight and dry from the rain. The introduction of walls would prevent any cross-ventilation.

There is insufficient in-depth research into the science of building in the tropics of Southeast Asia. This region is dissimilar to the African tropical belt or the tropical Indian sub-continent. Principles developed for use in Africa are not applicable here. The lack of any established local models is problematic for the foreign-trained Malaysian architect. A new set of rules and guidelines needs to be introduced for adoption. My work is an attempt to break away from existing accepted built forms, to try to overcome and provide answers to some of the contradictions which confront architects designing in the tropics. In all or most of the projects there is a deliberate attempt to do away with walls wherever possible.

The search for a solution to using more sustainable and renewable building materials has become a current area of interest, together with that of harnessing energy from nature. In the tropics we have lots of energy from the sun, it provides lighting, heating, as well as electricity from solar cells, rainwater, wind at high level, other mechanical devices to produce energy for the building's own use. An architectural form evolved from the above and totally dependent on nature for its own sustainability will be what we are looking for as an answer to tropical architecture.

The current way of designing high-rise buildings in the tropics may be out-dated. I see the future of tropical high-rise buildings not as "energy-chompers" but rather as "energy-towers" that are self-sustaining and also supplying energy to the surrounding neighbourhood. These towers should be the energy source of the district. Imagine the whole of Asia's tropical cities being covered by these "energy-towers". It will be a new architecture, a form still not seen before.

Ideally the tropical city should have an urban built-up that is set in a forest. If there are to be any tall buildings these tall buildings should be energy generators which are sustainable and will be obvious to even a casual observer that it is a building that has its origin in the tropics. Automobiles and other forms of combustion-engine driven vehicles should be permitted to be used with restrictions attached. Only non-pollutant means of transportation will be encouraged. With the restriction and control on automobiles there will not be any need for extensive road systems. This will release a lot of land now required to be set aside for roads. The total urbanscape will be different from the existing. This long-term sustainability of the city will provide man with a chance to regenerate resources which could otherwise be depleted rapidly.

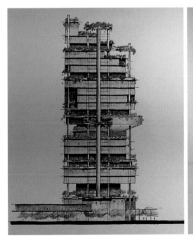

Pacific Bank front elevation and model

Sketch of a tropical energy city

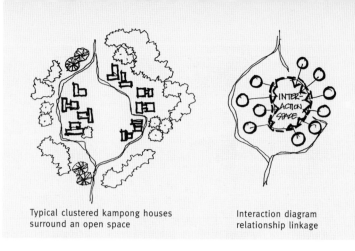

Typical clustered kampong houses
surround an open space

Interaction diagram
relationship linkage

A Tropical Solution to Sustainable Housing

Kampongminium (*kampong* and *condominium*). A marriage of the traditional Malay village (kampong) and the modern high-rise living of the condominiums. A marriage of modern and progressive residential, commercial and other facilities set in an inviting environmental context and the communal intimacy typical of a kampong.

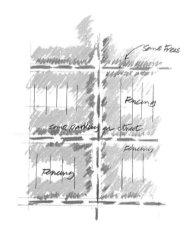

Usual housing layout on a grid pattern

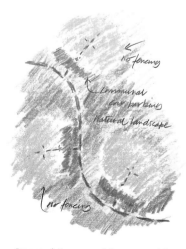

Proposed Kampongminium concept for a more environmental-friendly living

Typical elevation for Kampongminium

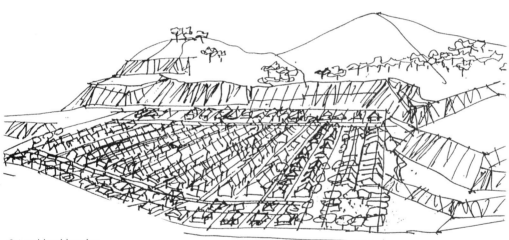

Cut and level housing

Kampongminium housing environment

207

Sen Kapadia

The New Vernacular

Architecture begins with functional and budgetary limits then assume character with the architect's material manifestations of these limits in aesthetic expression. Historically, this transformation reflected the region's materials, climate and local culture. However, in the face of rapid urbanisation, most Asian cities are changing that inner form in favour of an universal one; most of which are clad in glass and steel. This 'nowhere' architecture is genealogically unfit and spiritually bereft. In its fondness for newness, it discards old wisdom.

In response to abundant tropical natural light and ventilation as well as budgetary limitations, the Asian architect accepts the added responsibility of making his or her architecture energy-conscious. As a matter of fact, buildings utilising natural light and wind energy have proven to consume only half of the supplementary conventional energy for cooling and lighting. Energy-conscious architecture is easily replicable in the vast hinterlands of Asia.

Asian architecture is an emergent force, expressing contemporary universal aesthetics steeped in local traditional values by responding to the sun, the true giver of form (Image 1), wind, the life force (Image 2) and materials of the sacred earth. Built in the "new vernacular" language, it is at peace with inner and outer sensibilities.

सुर्य

1

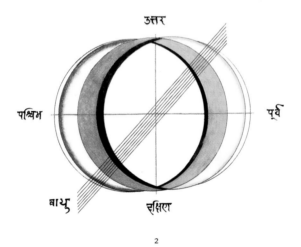

2

The ancient Indian discovery of *venturi* effect is an essential ingredient of the projects illustrated here. Image 3 shows an image called the "Gaumukhi", meaning cow-faced thus 'sacred', is deployed in plot selection and building orientation. Here, in windward direction, there is a smaller opening, whereas in the leeward direction, there is a larger opening. This configuration induces a perceptible current of air. The alternative in Image 4 suggests such configuration applied to the cross section of the building. On the other hand, Image 5 shows the reverse configuration with larger opening in the windward direction and a smaller opening in the leeward direction that inhibits the air circulation. Hence it is called "Waghmukhi", meaning tiger-faced and thus 'profane'.

The Asian culture has a profusion of colours that are derived from natural stones, vegetables and minerals and over the centuries, which are assigned significance through cultural and religious references. I like to recognise colours thus: the Hindu God, Krishna as blue and earth-red; the Hindu God, Shrinathji as black; Tulsi (sacred basil plant) as green and so on. Buildings replete with such hues are not just painted buildings, but enduring symbols of cultural memories.

There is a poignancy in responding to local climatic and cultural influences. The desirable south-west breeze, local colour sensibilities and subdued sunlight are most prominent influences on the two projects illustrated here. The skin of these projects is double-layered to offer deeply recessed windows that avoid glare and prevent heat gain. The orientation and plans are evolved to trap and distribute breeze and daylight. Finally, colours derived from Miniature paintings provide aesthetic clues.

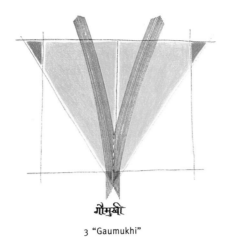

गौमुखी

3 "Gaumukhi"

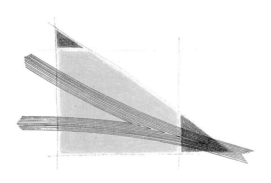

4

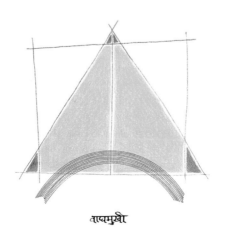

वाघमुखी

5 "Waghmukhi"

Sumeru Apartment Building
Mumbai, India, 1997.

Sumeru Apartment Building poses the question of the 'vertical neighbourhood'. Apartments stacked over each other do not encourage the making of a neighbourhood. Also, with the growing dependency on electronic communication, future apartments are likely to encourage working from home; one no longer has to leave home for work. Such apartments are anticipated to change the city pattern and demand more interactive buildings. Two options are studied and one of them is built in a suburb of Mumbai. This tower of grouped apartments is interspersed with meeting places on the eighth floor and the roof terrace, offering spaces for social interaction. Bathed in traditional colours, it proclaims its presence in the suburbs of Mumbai and claims its place in the etched memories of its occupants, at once new and familiar.

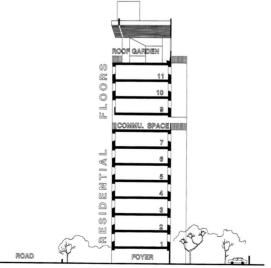

Cross section

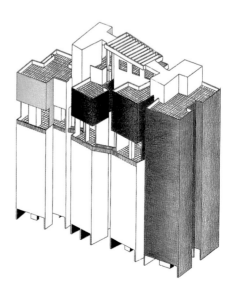

Eighth floor open public spaces for play

Eighth floor open public spaces for meetings

Twelfth floor terrace level meeting place

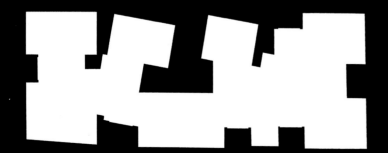

Organisational footprint of five apartments responsive to daylight and breeze
Typical floor plan

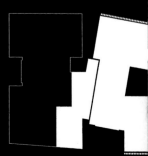

Communal space – ninth storey p

Close-up of communal spaces

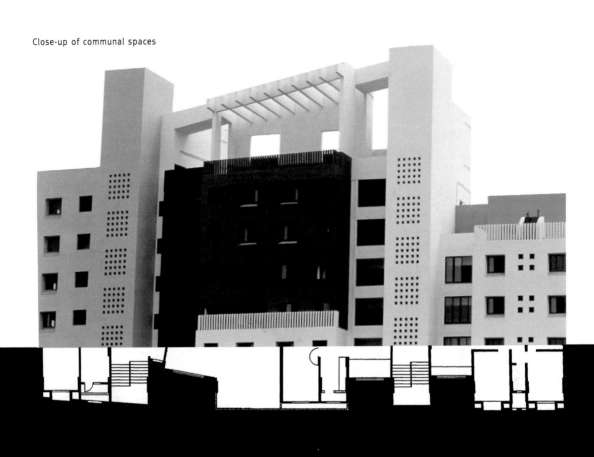

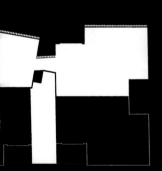

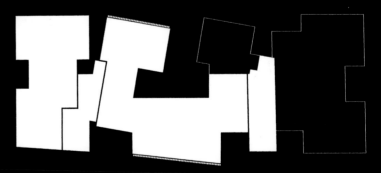

Roof top terrace conceived as a room without a roof – thirteenth storey plan

The Computer Science Building
Mumbai, India, 1994.

The Computer Science Building fits within the vast existing grid of covered corridors and as such, demands subdued external architectural characteristics. This building thus goes beyond the natural light/ventilation dialogue and goes on to subvert the external skin to a non-vocal envelop, highlighting the active central architectural interiors, filled with natural light and traditional colours.

Classrooms are located to the north to gain the gentle light and allow larger apertures to effect cross ventilation as in the 'Gaumukhi' concept discussed earlier. All floor trusses are assigned different colours to ensure separate identities for various areas within the building and to provide visual landmarks.

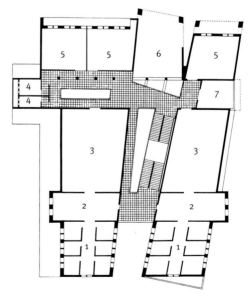

1 Faculty room
2 Research scholars
3 Research lab
4 Toilets
5 Classroom
6 Upper part of porch
7 Tea room

Third storey plan

0   5   10m

Our fundamental concern: an architectural identity which reflects the nuances of the local society and encapsulates these aspects: climate, technology and culture; there is a need to develop a uniquely Asian architecture in addition to being at the cutting edge of modern technology.

Sonny Chan Sau Yan

A Modern Architecture
for the Tropics

Wisma Selangor Dredging Complex
Kuala Lumpur. Malaysia. 1986.

The Wisma Selangor Dredging Complex in the early 1980s contrasts sharply with the previous "vernacular" approach. The design was inspired, in part, by Peter and Alison Smithson's Economist Building in London, and is broken down into four component towers surrounding open courtyard, all serviced by a common service core. The entire public circulation space at the ground level is naturally ventilated.

Typical plan   Roof plan

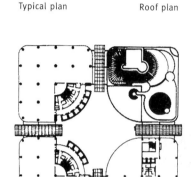
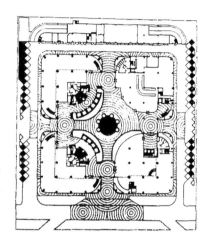

Typical plan   Fifth floor   First storey plan

No. 3C Tanglin Hill
Singapore. 1998.

In this house, extensive wide verandahs are used in the manner of old colonial bungalows, as a mediating space between the inside and the outside. Water bodies and lush landscaping throughout the compound help to reduce the radiant heat as well as to establish a sense of its "place" in the tropics.

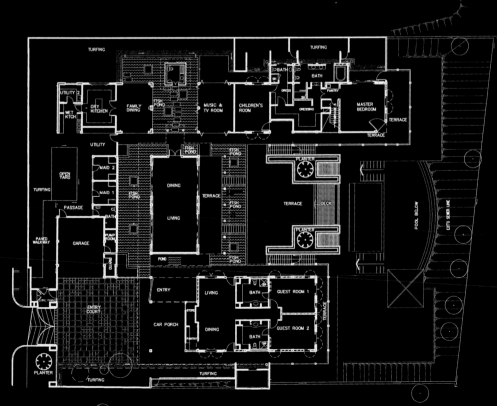

First storey plan

Nassim Jade Condominium
Singapore, 1997.

Nassim Jade is a more resolved example of a response to the tropical climate with the use of technology. It responds to the intrinsic factors of a modern building in a tropical environment. The focus of the U-shaped development centres around a richly landscaped courtyard and pool area. The surrounding buildings are encased in an interactive envelope, which works to provide privacy as well as shade. The screen is of timber louvres which are detached from the main structure. Nassim Jade is therefore "air-conditionable", as opposed to air-conditioned.

Longitudinal section

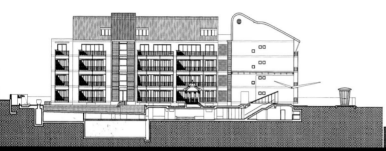
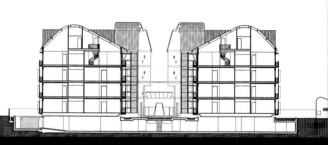

Nassim Road

First storey plan

| | |
0 1   10m

Bournemouth Eight Strata Bungalows
Singapore, 1998.

The blurring of definitions between the private and the public realms is explored in this group of bungalows. Privacy and identity versus community is carefully orchestrated through manipulations of architectural forms and strategies that suggest boundaries physical or otherwise. In the tropics, the relationship to the outside takes on an almost spiritual role beyond its pragmatic role of affording physiological comfort. Here it is recognised, articulated and investigated in a sophisticated manner within the tight constraints of its plot size and commercial viability.

Opposite: The swimming pool, defined by living area and side wall of the neighbouring bungalow, forms an ambiguous realm that is in between the inside and the outside, the private and the public.

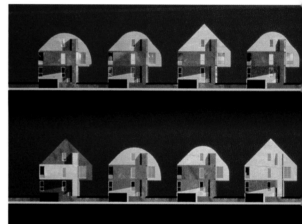

Section

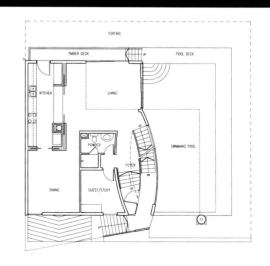

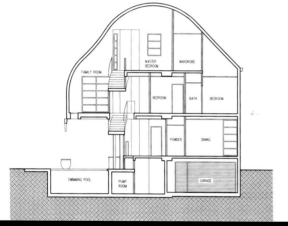

Basement plan

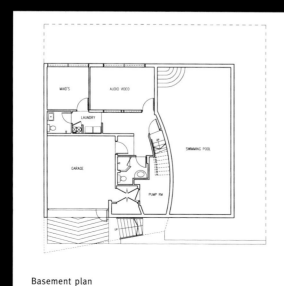

First storey plan

Second storey plan

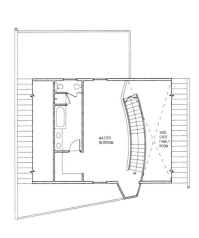

Attic plan

Maybank Competition,
Singapore, 1998.

The competition entry for the Maybank represents a first conscious attempt to design a "tropical" high-rise. The building has been designed for a very narrow site. The external environment is brought into the workplace at every opportunity. The banking hall is at the basement level and lit from the glazed pedestrian plaza above, allowing the lobby unrestricted views towards the river and the historical parts of the city beyond. The nine levels of office space above are all double-volume spaces with mezzanines and sky gardens on each floor allowing tenants to enjoy natural light and ventilation during their breaks. The exterior is clad in a marble perforated screen which is detached from the main structure and is reminiscent of the "Jali", pierced stone screens found in Islamic architecture. This shades the interior and provides a diffused light, which is enhanced by the double-height space and this in turn reduces the need for heavy air-conditioning.

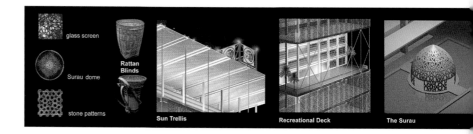

Day & night views

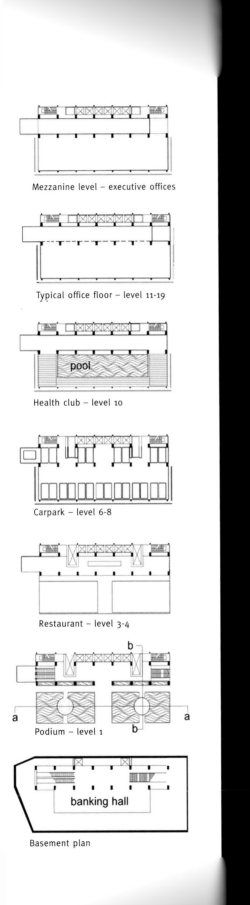

Mezzanine level – executive offices

Typical office floor – level 11-19

pool

Health club – level 10

Carpark – level 6-8

Restaurant – level 3-4

b

a ——————————————————— a

b

Podium – level 1

banking hall

Basement plan

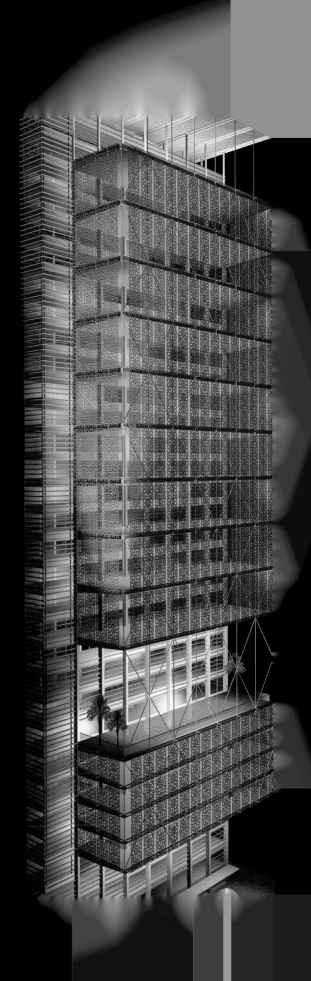

Biodata

Fumihiko Maki
(b. 1928)

Professor Maki is Principal of Maki and Associates, Tokyo (1965-). He lectures extensively in universities in the USA and his work is published in many monographs in Japanese, French and English. Maki was professor of the Department of Architecture, University of Tokyo, 1979-89.
He has won countless major domestic and international architectural project prizes and awards. For his outstanding contribution to architecture he is Honorary Fellow of Institutes of Architecture in the UK, the Czech Republic, Germany, France, the USA and Mexico.

Leon van Schaik
(b. 1944)

Professor Leon van Schaik is Dean of the Faculty of the Constructed Environment at RMIT. He studied at the AA School of Architecture in London and in turn taught and practised from that base, working in the early 1980's with the Urban Foundation in Soweto. He writes regularly for architec-tural and other journals focusing on urbanism, criticism and architecture as popular culture and is the Executive Editor of *Transition*. As an architect, he has worked on self-help and conventional housing; has designed and built complex educational buildings, art galleries and factories.

William S. W. Lim
(b. 1932)

A graduate of the Architectural Association (AA) London, he continued his graduate study at the Department of City and Regional Planning, Harvard University, as a Fullbright Fellow. He is the principal partner of William Lim Associates Pte whose main focus is idea innovation and design excellence. Lim writes and lectures. His recent books are: *Asian New Urbanism* (1998), *Contemporary Vernacular: Evoking Traditions in Asian Architecture* (1998). Lim is the President of AA Asia, a board member of LaSalle-SIA College of Fine Arts (Singapore) and an editorial board member of Solidarity-current affairs, ideas and the Arts (Manila). He is also Adjunct Professor of the RMIT, Australia and Guest Professor of Tianjin University, China.

Sumet Jumsai
(b. 1939)

Sumet Jumsai studied architecture and obtained a Ph.D. at Cambridge University from 1958 to 1967, and has been a faculty member of the Department of Architecture at Cambridge since 1991. His private practice based in Bangkok, which started in 1969, is responsible for over 200 projects. Besides numerous articles, he is also the author of a number of books, including *Naga: Cultural Origins in Siam and the West Pacific* (Oxford University Press, 1988). Jumsai was awarded the Cultural Award for art and culture at the World Economic Forum, Davos, 1999.

Wu Liangyong
(b. 1922)

Born in Nanjing, he graduated with a Bachelor of Architecture from the National Central University in Chongqing (China) and subsequently studied architecture under Eliel Saarinen at the Cranbrook Academy of Art, USA (1949). Professor Wu Liangyong is a well-known figure in China. He spreads his time between academia, practice and consultancy work to various local and central governments in China. He is currently Professor of Architecture at Tsinghua University.

Min Hyunsik
(b. 1946)

Min Hyunsik completed his undergraduate studies at the Seoul National University in 1970, and after many years of practice, went to the AA School of Architecture in London in 1990 for "retraining". In 1992, he established H. Min Architect & Associates based in Seoul. He has also guest lectured at the Seoul City University, Seoul National University, and is currently a professor at the Korean National University of Arts.

C. Anjalendran
(b. 1951)

C. Anjalendran graduated from the University College of London and attained his M. Sc. from the University of London. He has been in independent practice for 16 years and represented Sri Lanka at "Roots: Innovation and Tradition in Asian Architecture Today" at the Fujita Venta Museum, Tokyo in 1996.

Sardjono Sani
(b. 1963)

Sardjono Sani graduated from the University Catholic Parahyangan, Bandung (1987). In 1990 he completed his Master of Architecture at the University of Colorado, Denver, and won the Best Design Student Award. In 1992 he set up his own architectural practice: PT Bias Tekno-Art Kreasindo. Since 1993 Sardjono has held seven exhibitions in Indonesia, the USA and the Netherlands. Sardjono's works have been published in architectural journals and general magazines in Indonesia and abroad. Since 1994 Sardjono has been active in teaching.

Balkrishna Doshi
(b. 1927)

Balkrishna Doshi worked for Le Corbusier for four years in Paris before returning to India to start his own firm. Today he is the Founder-Director of institutions in Ahmedabad, which include the School of Architecture, the School of Planning, the Visual Arts Centre, and the Kanoria Centre for the Arts. Doshi has also been instrumental in establishing the research institute Vastu-Shilpa Foundation for Studies and Research in Environmental Design, which has done pioneering work in low cost housing and city planning.

Mathar Bunnag
(b. 1950)

Mathar Bunnag graduated from the University of Manitoba with a Master of Architecture, and went on to complete his Master of Architecture in Urban Design at the GSD, Harvard. He has lectured both at the School of Architecture, National University of Singapore (1984-1986) and the University of Hong Kong (1986-1988). In 1988, he started his own practice in Hong Kong and sub-sequently moved it back to Bangkok in 1990.

Hu Shyr-Fong
(b. 1956)

Hu Shyr-Fong was educated at the Department of Architecture, Tung-Hai University in Taiwan and obtained his Master of Architecture in Urban Design at the GSD, Harvard (MAUD). He started Shyr-Fong Design Studio in Taiwan after working for a few years both in Taiwan and the USA. He has lectured at the Department of Architecture and Department of Interior Design, Chung-Yuan University and the Department of Space Design, Shih-Jen College. In 1995, he wrote for several publications: *The Chinese Architect, The Dialogue,* and *The Interior* and authored *Observation of Cities and Architecture* (Chuanhsing Publishing Co., Ltd., 1996).

Jimmy C. S. Lim
(b. 1944)

Born in Penang and educated at the University of New South Wales, Australia, Lim returned in 1978 to Malaysia to start his own practice: CSL Associates. An active conservationist, he was a founder member of the Heritage of Malaysia Trust. He was also President of the Malaysian Institute of Architects (PAM) from 1991-1993, and Editor of *Majalah Akitek.* Lim has won numerous awards, the most recent being the Aga Khan Award for Architecture (1998). Known for his tropical architecture he gives public lectures, talks and teaches at universities locally and internationally.

Sen Kapadia
(b. 1936)

Graduated from the Sir J. J.
College of Architecture
in Mumbai in 1962,
Sen Kapadia worked briefly
with Louis Khan in
Philadelphia in 1964. He has
established his own practice
since 1980 in Mumbai, and
in 1995 was awarded the
Indian Institute of Architects
Annual Award for Excellence
in Design.

Sonny Chan Sau Yan
(b. 1941)

Educated at the Northern
Polytechnic in London, he
proceeded to immerse
himself in the discourse
about Tropical Architecture in
the 60s at the AA School of
Architecture. Upon his return
to Singapore, he joined
Kumpulan Akitek and left in
1993 to set up his own
practice – Chan Sau Yan
Associates. His project, the
Bournemouth Eight strata
housing won him a
Singapore Institute of
Architects Architectural
Design Award in 1998.
From 1987 to 1990,
he was Adjunct Associate
Professor at the School of
Architecture, National
University of Singapore.

Tan Kok Meng
(b. 1964)

Graduated from the School
of Architecture, National
University of Singapore
with top honours in 1992.
He has been a part-time
lecturer at both RMIT/LaSalle-
SIA College of the Arts
(Interior Architecture) and
the National University of
Singapore. Currently, he
is the Chief Editor of the
Singapore Architect journal,
and a Masters candidate
at the Centre de Cultura
Contemporania in Barcelona.

Acknowledgements

Photo & Illustration Credits	Page
Art4d	54-55, 64-65
SJA+3D	62
A. Kamprasert	63
Kim Yongkwan	97 (right), 99, 103
Park Youngchea	105
Channa Daswatte	106, 112-119
S. Dharmavasan	108-111
Roy Genggam/LARAS	120 (first photo from left), 123-125
Oki Soetrisno/LARAS	120 (photos 2, 3 and 4 from left), 126-129
Yatin Pandya	cover, 141 (left), 142-144, 145 (right), 148, 152-153, 156
John Panikar	141 (right), 145 (left), 146-147
Atul Kantekar and Mahendra More	155 (illustration/drawing)
Robert Powell	193 (section), 203
B. S. Kumar	215
Albert Lim	224-227

The publisher also wishes to thank
the architects, photographers and all who
have contributed so much to make
this publication possible.

s t o n e w o r k

stone...

an essence of modern living space

BUILDERS SHOP PTE LTD
魯班行

11 changi south street 3 builders centre singapore 486122 tel 545 5225 fax 545 5665 email sales@buildershop.com.sg

glass mosaics • tiles • marbles • silica agglomerates • quartzites • limestone • sandstone •
granite • pebbles • laminated floors • sealers & stonecare products

Select Books is a publisher, distributor and bookseller specialising in books on Southeast Asia.

Other books on architecture available at Select Books:

An Alternative Urban Strategy
William S. W. Lim

The Asian House: Contemporary Houses of Southeast Asia
Robert Powell

Asian New Urbanism
William S. W. Lim

Cities for People: Reflections of a Southeast Asian Architect
William S. W. Lim

Contemporary Vernacular: Conceptions and Perceptions
Christopher Chew (ed)

Contemporary Vernacular: Evoking Traditions in Asian Architecture
William S. W. Lim and Tan Hock Beng

Equity and Urban Environment in the Third World: with special reference to Asean countries and Singapore
William S. W. Lim

Innovative Architecture of Singapore
Robert Powell

Land for Housing the Poor
S. Angel (ed)

Living Legacy: Singapore's Architectural Heritage Renewed
Robert Powell

Pastel Portraits: Singapore's Architectural Heritage
Gretchen Liu

Through the Floating World: Architectural Impressions of Japan
Tan Kok Meng (ed)

The Tropical Asian House
Robert Powell

The Urban Asian House: Living in Tropical Cities
Robert Powell

For more information, please contact:
Select Books Pte Ltd
19 Tanglin Road
#03-15 Tanglin Shopping Centre
Singapore 247909
Tel: (65) 732 1515   Fax: (65) 736 0855
Email: selectbk@cyberway.com.sg